Strategic and Performance Management of Olympic Sport Organisations

Jean-Loup Chappelet • Emmanuel Bayle

Master Exécutif en Management des Organisations Sportives
Executive Masters in Sports Organisation Management

**HUMAN
KINETICS**

Library of Congress Cataloging-in-Publication Data

Chappelet, J.-L. (Jean-Loup)
   Strategic and performance management of Olympic sport organisations
/ Jean-Loup Chappelet, Emmanuel Bayle.
      p. cm.
   Includes bibiographical references.
   ISBN 0-7360-5829-X (soft cover)
   1. Sports administration--Europe. 2. Sports--Europe--Societies, etc.
3. Olympics.   I. Bayle, Emmanuel, 1970-   . II. Title.
GV713.C47 2004
796'.06'9--dc22

2004016500

ISBN-10: 0-7360-5829-X
ISBN-13: 978-0-7360-5829-2

The Web addresses cited in this text were current as of July 19, 2004, unless otherwise noted.

Acquisitions Editor: Myles Schrag
Managing Editor: Lee Alexander
Copyeditor: Joyce Sexton
Permission Manager: Dalene Reeder
Graphic Designer: Nancy Rasmus
Graphic Artist: Tara Welsch
Cover Designer: Keith Blomberg
Photographer (cover): Acestock/Robertstock
Art Manager: Kareema McLendon
Illustrator: Tara Welsch
Printer: United Graphics

Printed in the United States of America   10 9 8 7 6 5 4 3

Human Kinetics
Web site: www.HumanKinetics.com

United States: Human Kinetics
P.O. Box 5076
Champaign, IL 61825-5076
800-747-4457
e-mail: humank@hkusa.com

Canada: Human Kinetics
475 Devonshire Road, Unit 100
Windsor, ON N8Y 2L5
800-465-7301 (in Canada only)
e-mail: info@hkcanada.com

Europe: Human Kinetics
107 Bradford Road
Stanningley
Leeds LS28 6AT, United Kingdom
+44 (0)113 255 5665
e-mail: hk@hkeurope.com

Australia: Human Kinetics
57A Price Avenue
Lower Mitcham, South Australia 5062
08 8372 0999
e-mail: info@hkaustralia.com

New Zealand: Human Kinetics
Division of Sports Distributors NZ Ltd.
P.O. Box 300 226 Albany
North Shore City, Auckland
0064 9 448 1207
e-mail: info@humankinetics.co.nz

Contents

Part I Strategic Management of Olympic Sport Organisations

by Jean-Loup Chappelet, IDHEAP

Foreword

Sport is playing an increasingly important role in a world of changing economic, political, cultural, and social systems. A new context for sport is being developed around the globe, providing an extraordinary opportunity to discover and take advantage of the sports experience of many countries, and in doing so, to improve the management of sport organisations.

One of the greatest challenges for sport bodies is ensuring that their current and future managers have the necessary skills to lead their organisations in the twenty-first century. In order to function most effectively, sport organisations require an increasing comprehension of international sport issues, in addition to those of strategic management, performance, marketing, and human resources.

Facing their daily challenges, Olympic sports organizations (OSOs) have accumulated successful (and less successful) experiences, and their managers have gained competences enabling them to efficiently run their organisations. The MEMOS programme has been established on the understanding that cooperation between those managers and scholars on the management of OSOs could be the base of what we might call an "Olympic learning community" that is able to gather, formalise, implement, and disseminate that specific management knowledge and know-how.

MEMOS was founded in 1995 upon the initiative of several European national Olympic committees, the European Network of Sport Sciences in Higher Education, several universities and schools of sport, and with the financial support of Olympic Solidarity and the Socrates programme of the European Union. The aim of MEMOS was to provide a higher level of training for European sport managers. MEMOS soon after began to attract sport managers from other continents, and in the summer of 2002, the MEMOS Steering Committee decided to open and adapt the programme to international participation.

The MEMOS curriculum consists of three one-week residential modules, each of 6 intensive days, scheduled over an academic year together with distance learning and the development of a personal project. Each module takes place in a different city and is placed under the joint responsibility of a scholar and a professional sport manager. The first module usually takes place in Lausanne, the Olympic capital city. During the course of their study year, the participants undertake a project concerning the management of a sport organisation, in principle the one in which they are active. The last two days of each module are dedicated to the coaching of the participants for their projects. The public presentation of these projects and the awarding of the degrees take place at the Olympic Museum in Lausanne. Since its creation, more than 200 managers operating in international or national OSOs worldwide have been awarded the MEMOS degree.

The idea of creating a series of textbooks ("MEMOS manuals") is perfectly in line with the MEMOS project but introduces a further step in its development. It gives the opportunity to a broader audience to have access to the ongoing process of the "Olympic learning community" and to widely disseminate the fundamental basis and main findings of a

10-year experience that has brought together OSO managers and academics.

Choosing strategy and performance as the first topic for these MEMOS manuals could be seen both as logical and challenging. It is logical because identifying and formulating a mission, conducting an assessment of external threats/opportunities and internal strengths/weaknesses, defining goals and steps to reach them, evaluating the results of undertaken actions are indeed the conditions to start a well-thought managerial approach in OSOs. It is challenging because such a strategic and performance process has to be adapted to the context of voluntarily led organisations with strong traditions and habits.

Jean-Loup Chappelet, the current MEMOS director, has a long experience as a manager in OSOs and is now a professor at the Swiss Graduate School of Public Administration associated with the University of Lausanne. He is in the best position to write such a book. His co-writer, Emmanuel Bayle, associate professor at the Claude Bernard University of Lyon, France, has been working for 10 years on the performance of sports organisations in a long-term collaboration with the French National Olympic Committee. Both of them, through the MEMOS programme, have coached many MEMOS participants working on the evaluation and improvement of the functioning of their OSOs.

For all these reasons I am strongly supporting the publication of their book and see it as a cornerstone for the development of the management of Olympic sport organizations.

Professor Jean Camy
Claude Bernard University of Lyon, France
MEMOS Founder and first Director

Preface to
« Strategic and Performance Management of Olympic Sports Organisations »

We are currently living in a golden age of sport. Never, since ancient times, has sport occupied as important a place in society as it does today. This status has been won throughout the 20th century by athletes themselves inspired by sporting excellence, particularly that of the Olympic Games.

A pyramid of association-style organisations has gradually formed, from the local club to the national Olympic committee, passing through regional leagues and national federations, up to the international sport federations and Olympic Games organising committees. The leaders of these "Olympic Sport Organisations" are essentially volunteers, who perform their functions by drawing on their professional expertise, which is often wide-ranging.

In the 21st century the general administration and daily running of sport require increasingly specific knowledge. To preserve and maintain this golden age of sport, the leaders of the volunteer sports movement must become more professional. They must familiarize themselves with management techniques and adapt them to the sporting phenomenon which they know so well. They must also learn to work with salaried managers who understand the specificities of sport and share their managerial language.

For the last twenty years or so, high-level athletes have no longer been amateurs in the sense of dabblers. They have become professionals, that is to say experts who like and fully master their sports technique. The same must be true of sports administrators and policy-makers who nowadays manage considerable human, financial and material resources, and have great responsibilities such as educating young people, public health and social inclusiveness.

Sport needs managers from within its ranks who can plan their organisation's strategy and steer its performance. For this reason, and as one of the first supporters of the MEMOS programme, I welcome the publication of this book, hoping that it will contribute to a better understanding of sport management, as well as a better strategic and performance management of Olympic sport organisations throughout the world.

Juan Antonio SAMARANCH
Honorary President for Life of the
International Olympic Committee

Introduction

Sport—a force within education, health, economic development, the labour market, social issues, national cohesion and identity—is increasingly taking the form of a tool for development on an educational, social, economic, urban planning, and image level for nations. It is no surprise to see the jealousies and control that it engenders relating not only to public policies but also to the practices of companies that position themselves in the sport sector (event organisation, leisure sport) or that use sport as a communications platform (sponsoring, philanthropy, etc.).

Nevertheless, sport is historically managed by associative organisations that belong to the sport and Olympic movement. These organisations form part of a wider movement, the "tertiary sector," whose political, economic, and social importance has grown constantly over the last 20 years in developed countries. They have a specific management framework: voluntary work by those at their head, a democratic method of functioning, and a nonprofit basis of operation.

The principles, conditions, and methods of management must take these characteristics into consideration and function accordingly. We thus think that responding to two questions is essential: How should the nature of the performance that such organisations seek to achieve be evaluated, and how should this performance be driven?

Confronted with an environment that has changed considerably (in terms of greater competitiveness, professionalisation), most Olympic sport organisations (OSOs; i.e., organisations that belong to the Olympic system and to the sport movement: clubs, national sport federations, international federations, national Olympic committees, organising committees) have progressed from an administrative logic to a marketing approach and then to a strategic one. The strategic and performance management approach aims to define a project, to structure it in a way that will permit it to be successful, and then to evaluate it once it is completed in order to draw useful conclusions for the continuation of this project or development of new ones.

The purpose of this work is, in precise terms, to highlight the new issues at stake, the principles, and the methods that the OSOs must be aware of and implement in order to define their strategy and pilot their performance. The data and analyses presented herein come from case studies of OSOs and research into OSOs, notably in European countries.

The work comprises two parts. The first presents application of the strategic approach to OSOs and gives numerous examples of forms this can take. The second part raises issues regarding ways of evaluating the performance of the OSOs and proposes a framework that makes it possible to understand the key elements of strategy and steering.

Jean-Loup Chappelet and Emmanuel Bayle
Lausanne and Lyon, April 2004

Strategic Management of Olympic Sport Organisations

Jean-Loup Chappelet
IDHEAP Swiss Graduate School of Public Administration, Lausanne, Switzerland

As the bibliography for part I indicates, dozens of books and hundreds of articles have been written on strategic management. There is even a scientific journal exclusively devoted to the subject: *The Strategic Management Journal.* Strategy and management constitute an inevitable tandem. Outstanding authors have approached this natural union and have considered it for all kinds of organisations: large and small, private and public, and either nonprofit or profit making.

The purpose of this first part is not, of course, to propose totally new ideas on the subject, nor is it an attempt to sum up all these works, even though the main authors dealing with the various sectors are quoted. The aim is more simply to present a clear idea of what strategic management represents and how this can be applied with the help of various practical tools in the "amateur" sport sector. Several cases of practical approaches within sport organisations belonging to the Olympic system are presented. This system, which unites the organisations to a varying extent in preparing and running the Olympic Games, is briefly introduced in chapter 3. We call these organisations, such as the International

Olympic Committee (IOC), national Olympic committees (NOCs), international sport federations (IFs), national sport federations (NFs), and organising committees (OCOGs), Olympic sport organisations or OSOs.

Olympic sport organizations belong, in fact, to the world of nonprofit organisations (NPOs), that is, organisations whose main goal is not financial returns but the performance of their (ideal) mission. Nonprofits can make a profit, but should use this profit to further the activities they organise for their members instead of sharing it among their owners or shareholders. Moreover, NPOs have members and stakeholders rather than customers and clients; they depend on many volunteers, usually have a two-level governance made up of elected officials and hired managers, and also are more open to public-opinion scrutiny ("publicness") than the for-profit commercial companies.

Nonprofit organisations constitute the bulk of sport organisations from the local sport clubs to the international federations and the International Olympic Committee, through the regional sport amateur leagues and national governing bodies. These organisations belong to the world of so-called amateur sport, in contrast to professional (team) sport, which exists in many developed countries. Many authors also consider the public sector organisations (and hence governmental sport bodies such as offices, councils, ministries) as nonprofits (see, for example, Kotler and Andreasen 1991, p. 10). In fact, nonprofit organisations can have many kinds of legal status: associations, foundations, cooperatives, trusts, societies, and even (not-for-profit) corporations and companies.

Although several works on strategic management in the nonprofit organisations exist (see the bibliography), none are specifically devoted to sport organisations. A forerunner (in French) is the book published in 1989 by Ramanantsoa and Thiery-Baslé, which includes a chapter on the strategy of French national sport federations or governing bodies. The chapter "Strategy in Sport Organizations" from Slack's textbook *Understanding Sport Organizations* (1997) mainly covers entities from the commercial sector and not OSOs. Cases in the noncommercial sector are rarely described, even though these organisations are more and more using a strategic approach.

A second objective of part I (chapters 1 to 4) is thus to reveal how the concepts and tools of strategic management can be applied to entities within the Olympic system, taking into account their specific characteristics and their environment steeped in the context of world sport,

which is undergoing considerable evolution at the beginning of the 21st century and which sometimes is blurring the difference between amateur and professional sport.

The second part on performance management follows this first one quite naturally because, as we shall discover, although it is essential to define one's (strategic) objectives and plans, it is equally essential to verify the extent to which these have been achieved, with the purpose of improving the organisation's global managerial process. In fact, management can be considered a cyclical process consisting of three subprocesses that follow from each other (figure A): Strategic management is followed by operational management of the resources available to the sport organisation (in particular financial, human, and information resources) and finally performance management.

The subprocess of performance management serves to improve or correct strategic and operational management, depending on the situation, with the knowledge that it is sometimes extremely difficult to separate the strategic orientations from operational decisions and that the choice of performance indicators can also prove highly strategic. This statement is intended to reaffirm that management remains a global process and that the aim of dividing it into three subprocesses is above all a pedagogical one.

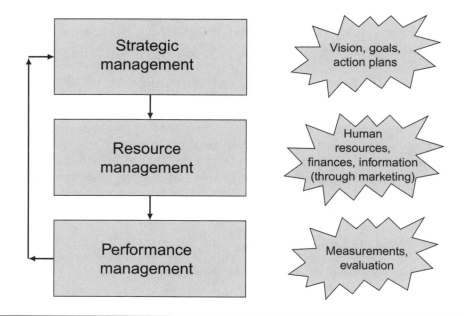

Figure A The three subprocesses of the management process.

one

Definition of Strategic Management

Speaking tautologically, we can define strategic management as the establishment and implementation of a strategy by managers. This definition, of course, requires added precision: Within a managerial framework, what exactly does a strategy constitute?

The idea of strategy as such comes from the military sectors: The Greek word *strategos* was a title for a general elected to protect a Greek city. Napoleon is said to have stated, very aptly, "Strategy is an art whose essence lies in its execution." Works by the Chinese general Sun Zu, the German Clausewitz, or the Swiss Jomini have long served as inspiration to those interested in strategy in a civilian framework.

Strategy as a theme became popular in companies during the 1960s with the development of competition among large firms. Following, in chronological order, are some definitions of company strategy found in literature, beginning with Chandler (one of the seminal authors in this field) in a 1962 book titled *Strategy and Structure*. "Strategy can be defined as the determination of the basic long-term goals and objectives of an enterprise and the adoption of courses of action and the allocation of resources necessary for carrying out these goals" (Chandler 1962, p. 13). Ansoff, in one of the great classics of management, says, "Strategy is viewed as an 'operator' which is designed to transform the firm from the present position to the position described by the objectives, subject to the constraints of the capabilities and the potential" (Ansoff 1965, p. 205). For Ansoff, contrary to Chandler, internal evolution can precede external change, and strategic management precisely consists of anticipating the structures that will be needed by a company to cope with change, and not only of adapting them to outside constraints (mainly competition).

One of the most influential authors in this field is undoubtedly Porter with his work *Competitive Strategy,* published for the first time in 1980, reprinted 57 times, and translated into 19 languages. Very much influenced by the art of warfare, he defines a (competitive) strategy as "taking offensive or defensive actions to create a defendable position in an industry, to cope successfully with competitive forces and thereby yield a superior return on investment for the firm" (Porter 1980, p. 34). "Competitive strategy is a combination of the *ends* (goals) for which the firm is striving and the *means* (policies) by which it is seeking to get there. Different firms have different words. . . . For example, some firms use terms like 'mission' or 'objectives' instead of 'goals' and some firms use 'tactics' instead of 'operating' or 'functional policies.' Yet the essential notion of strategy is captured in the distinction between the ends and means" (Porter 1980, p. xvi).

Following on from these various authors, a distinction was made between corporate (grand) strategy and business (divisional) strategy. Corporate strategy determines the company's fields of activity. This is what leads the company to become involved in or withdraw from a given sector in order to balance its portfolio of activities. Four types of corporate strategy are usually defined: growth, stability, defensive, and combination strategies. Business strategy is applied to each area of activity that is retained. It defines the manoeuvres that the company must accomplish in order to achieve a favourable positioning among its competitors in these areas (Strategor 1997, p. 9). Porter identifies three business strategies that a manager may choose: cost leadership, differentiation, and focus. For a more detailed explanation, see Slack (1997, p. 100). These concepts can be particularly well applied within the framework of top-down macro-analyses that are prepared to question the company as a whole and to redefine its products or services. Top-down analyses are conducted by high-level managers and consultants without much input from the lower-level employees.

This lack of participation of staff members is certainly a weakness if one considers the work by Crozier and Friedberg (1977) that developed in Europe in parallel to Porter's ideas. From their landmark book titled *L'acteur et le système (The Actors and the System)* stems what came to be known as "strategic analysis." This is a bottom-up approach to organisations (and not only those of a commercial nature) that takes into account (micro-) strategies on the part of actors who work in them or who influence them indirectly to a great extent. In fact, the actors all have their own objectives and projects, which are not necessarily compatible with those of the organisation but which are nevertheless essential to bear in mind when one is setting up or successfully implementing a global strategy. "The actors, if they wish to win or at least to minimise their losses, are forced to develop a 'winning' strategy. . . . This means that it is thus rational for them to conform to the requirements of the [organisational] game and for them to reach a point where they

subscribe to common goals, whatever their original motivations" (Crozier and Friedberg 1977, p. 230). In this way, these authors and their school of thinking see strategic analysis as an indispensable, complementary addition to the global systemic analysis of the organisation. These ideas are in part taken up within the notion of stakeholders, since the major stakeholders of any organisation include its staff and its managers (the main actors of the enterprise seen as a system).

During the 1970s and 1980s, the idea of strategy became closely linked to that of planning within the concept of strategic planning, as inherited from the managerial ideas of the period following World War II. Goodstein et al., for example, stated, "We define strategic planning as the process by which the guiding members of an organization envision its future and develop the necessary procedures and operations to achieve that future" (Goodstein et al. 1992, p. 1). According to Chelladurai (2001, p. 128), strategic planning is sometimes termed strategic management. Its main goal is to formulate a (strategic) plan.

In the 1990s, the concept of strategy was increasingly criticised, because with the acceleration within business some people thought that there was no longer time to plan a long-term strategy, that it was sufficient to be reactive, and that in a business environment the only possible strategy was to make profits. Porter responded as follows: "Strategy is the creation of a unique and valuable position, involving a different set of activities. If there were only one ideal position, there would be no need for strategy. . . . The essence of strategic positioning is to choose activities that are different from a rival's" (Porter 1995, p. 62).

In a famous essay published in 1994, *The Rise and Fall of Strategic Planning*, Mintzberg suggests that strategic planning is an oxymoron (p. 321) since it is impossible to plan objectives and decisions that must to some extent be adapted to the circumstances encountered by companies within an evolving market. This author does see strategy as a plan, but also in the form of four other facets, all beginning with a "P": Ploy, Pattern, Position, Perspective. These are Mintzberg's 5 Ps, which are nearly as famous as Philip Kotler's 4 Ps (product, price, promotion, and place) of a marketing mix.

Strategy is a *plan*—some sort of consciously intended course of action, a guideline (or set of guidelines) to deal with a situation. By this definition strategies have two essential characteristics: They are made in advance of the actions to which they apply, and they are developed consciously and purposefully.

As plan, a strategy can be a *ploy* too, which is really just a specific manoeuvre intended to outwit an opponent or competitor. If strategies can be intended (whether as general plans or specific ploys), they can also be realised. In other words, defining strategy as a plan is not sufficient; we also need a definition that encompasses the resulting behaviour, whether or not intended.

The definitions of strategy as plan and *pattern* can be quite independent of one another: Plans may go unrealised, while patterns may appear without preconception. Plans are intended strategy, whereas patterns are achieved strategy; from this we can distinguish deliberate strategies, where intentions that previously existed were achieved, and emergent strategies, where patterns developed either in the absence of intentions or despite them.

Strategy is also a *position*—specifically a means of locating an organisation in an "environment." By this definition strategy becomes the mediating force, or "match," between organisation and environment, that is, between the internal and external context.

Finally, strategy can be seen as a *perspective*—its content consisting not just of a chosen position but also of an ingrained way of perceiving the world. Strategy in this respect is to the organisation what personality is to the individual. What is of key importance is that strategy is a perspective shared by members of an organisation, through their intentions, or by their actions, or both. In effect, when we talk of strategy in this context, we are entering the realm of the collective mind—individuals united by common thinking or behaviour (or both).

Finally, for Slack, "Strategy may be planned and deliberate, it may emerge as a stream of significant decisions, or it may be some combination of both. In any of these situations organizational decision makers base their choice of strategy on their perceptions of the opportunities and threats in the environment, and the internal strengths and weaknesses of their organizations" (Slack 1997, p. 93). Figure 1.1 shows how achieving a strategy can be influenced by emergent strategies resulting from rapid types of evolution on the part of the environments and of the organisation's stakeholders.

Although during the 1990s strategic planning was criticised and thus somewhat neglected in the private sector, its use began in the third sector and also in the public sector. In one of the first works on the subject, Nutt and Backoff

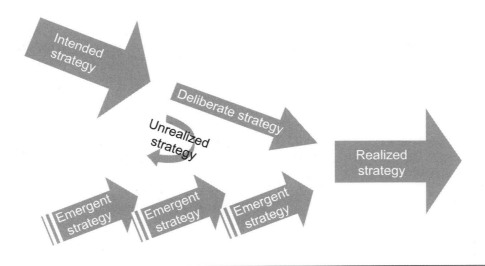

Figure 1.1 From intended to realized strategies.

stress "the importance of strategy in the public and nonprofit sectors" because of "turbulent conditions that were forcing change" (1992, pp. 1-2). For Joyce, "the formal system of strategic management in the public sector has emerged only recently and is based on strategic planning principles" (Joyce 2000, p. 3). Crozier affirms that in the public sector "a movement of reform can only develop based on the vision of a different future and by affirming some strong directions," in other words by "drawing up a strategy, a choice of priorities depending upon reasonable reflection regarding resources, constraints and objectives" (Crozier 1991, p. 196).

Oster devotes an entire book to strategic management for nonprofit organisations, although without mentioning sport organisations among the numerous cases presented (Oster 1995, p. ix). Most sport organisations, however, are nonprofit organisations (and in general, associations or foundations), meaning that their executives are not entitled to share in the profits as are shareholders in a private company. In a work that was a forerunner of its kind, Ramanantsoa and Thiery-Baslé acknowledged that the term strategy was absent (at the time) from the language used by the executives of sport organisations, but argued that these executives could not ignore the concept if they wished to adapt to the evolution of sport and how it is practised (1989, p. 23).

For these various authors, however, strategic management in nonprofit (or public) organisations is different from that in the commercial sector (see, for example, Nutt and Backoff 1992, p. 22). The main reason is that nonprofit organisations have a "publicness" that is (much) greater than that of organisations whose aim is to make a profit. We have of course seen, for example, that the International Olympic Committee crisis in 1999 aroused public interest to a far greater extent than if the case had been one of bribes within a simple, commercial firm. Indeed the "publicness" of

the International Olympic Committee is greater than that of many public organisations. (For a discussion of the concept of "publicness," see Bozeman 1987.)

These nonprofit organisations must have better accountability and legitimacy than organisations that make a profit, because the public idealises them. They must exercise concern regarding their many stakeholders (who have objectives that are unclear and sometimes diverging), while purely commercial organisations must first and foremost take care of their shareholders/owners and of their clients, since their main goal is to achieve profits. Nonprofit organisations must also take into account the fact that their standards of efficiency, effectiveness, performance, and allocated resources are not (and cannot be) exactly the same as in the commercial sector (see Part II). Their long-term goal is an ideal. They have a political dimension. Usually, there is no market for judging the success or the failure of a strategy. They have little competition. Moreover, numerous volunteers work within nonprofit organisations, often as elected officials who, in principle, decide on the strategy to be followed. Their motivations and opinions may be different from those of the salaried managers who are responsible for carrying out the strategy but who often also draw it up.

These differences do not, however, prevent application of the concepts and tools of strategic management to nonprofit organisations in general and to sport organisations such as clubs or national and international federations, and Olympic sport organizations in particular. It is simply a question of doing so intelligently, which means taking into account the major differences and not applying those tools that would be counterproductive. This is what we shall attempt to do in the following chapter, which proposes a way of establishing a strategy and of implementing it for nonprofit sport organisations.

two

The Process of Strategic Management and Its Practical Tools

Following on from Mintzberg's 5 Ps, intended to provide a better grasp of what a strategy means, it is possible to add a sixth P in order to stress that strategic management is above all a process that should be carried out: one of the three subprocesses of the managerial process (see figure A on p. 2). Most authors, moreover, propose sequential or cyclical models of this process based on stages, phases, or tasks. They vary simply with respect to the nature of these stages and their order. The number of stages is also variable depending on whether or not these models include operational management and performance management within the process.

Slack (1997, p. 103), for example, proposes the following stages in two phases:

- Strategy formulation phase:
  - Formulate a mission statement
  - Analyse the external environment and internal operations
  - Make choices about appropriate strategies
- Strategy implementation: choose an appropriate organisational structure and control systems

Nutt and Backoff (1992, p. 167) call for moving through six stages:

- Historical context
- Situational assessment
- Strategic issues tension agenda
- Strategic options
- Feasibility assessment
- Implementation

The Canadian International Development Agency (CIDA) pushes for a six-step strategic planning process (CIDA 1997, p.12) especially developed for (Canadian) nongovernmental organisations:

- Preparing the strategic planning process
- Analysing the organisation's internal environment
- Analysing the organisation's external environment
- Evaluating organisational capability
- Determining strategic objectives
- Action plan

Oster (1995, p. 12) proposes that a nonprofit organisation wanting to launch into strategic management proceed as follows:

- Establish a mission
- Carry out a global analysis of the sector of activity
- Study the nearby external environment
- Define the goals and objectives
- Identify the gap between the resources available and the resources necessary to achieve the objectives
- Carry out a strategy for reducing the gap
- Evaluate the results

Goodstein et al. (1992, p. 3) present a model involving nine sequential phases in three major stages:

- Setting the stage for planning:
  - Planning to plan
  - Values scan
  - Mission formulation
- Setting strategic directions:
  - Strategic business modelling
  - Performance audit
  - Gap analysis
- Implementation:
  - Integrating action plans
  - Contingency planning
  - Implementation

Kotler and Andreasen (1991, p. 69) adopt a classic model to propose their SMPP (Strategic Marketing Planning Process) for nonprofit organisations:

- Analyse organisation:
  - Mission, objectives, goals, culture
  - Strengths, weaknesses
- Analyse external environment:
  - Publics to be served
  - Competition
  - Social, political, technical, economic macro-environment
- Set marketing mission, objectives, and goals:
- Set core marketing strategy and marketing mix
- Set specific tactics and determine performance benchmarks

- Implement strategy
- Assess performance

Mintzberg (1994, p. 40) is somewhat scornful of these ever more complex models, notably that by Ansoff, containing no fewer than 57 steps. He considers designing strategy as a black box (p. 331) inserted within a network of activities that are the responsibility of the planners. These activities are the following:

- Strategic analysis
- Strategy formation
- Codifying strategies into plans
- External communication and control
- Internal communication and control

Without denying the importance of communication intended for target publics, stakeholders, and the staff of an organisation (the main utility of strategic plans according to Mintzberg), we shall concentrate on the first three activities listed above. We propose a simple, pragmatic model directly inspired by original ideas on designing strategy practised during the 1970s at the Harvard Business School. It is based on four questions that can be placed in a circle (see figure 2.1)

For each of these questions, there is a corresponding answer that must be supplied by those who wish to carry out strategic management (and performance management).

ANALYSIS:

| Where are we now? | External and internal analysis (step 1) |

VISION:

| Where do we want to be? | (New) vision, mission, and objectives (step 2) |

ACTION:

| How do we get there? | Strategies and tactics (step 3) |

CONTROL:

| Are we getting there? | Benchmarks and indicators (step 4) |

We shall now explore the stages that should make it possible to obtain these answers thanks to collective brainstorming. A whole series of creative techniques and intellectual tools are

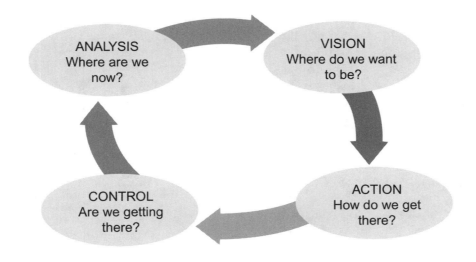

Figure 2.1 The strategic (and performance) management circle.

available to facilitate this process (see, for example, www.mindtools.com).

2.1 Internal and External Analysis (Step 1)

Analysing the strengths and weaknesses of an organisation and the opportunities and threats that its environment creates is, for many authors, synonymous with strategic analysis. This analysis is universally known by its acronym SWOT (Strengths, Weaknesses, Opportunities, and Threats). Nutt and Backoff make considerable use of this formulation when giving their definition of "strategic management [which] is a movement toward our mission, built upon an understanding of our current situation and an identification of our desired future, which permits us to build on our strengths, overcome our weaknesses, exploit our opportunities and block or blunt our threats" (1992, p. 437).

Opportunities (respectively, threats) are usually defined as positive (negative) environmental factors. Strengths are activities that the organisation does well or resources it controls. *Strengths* can be defined as one or more skills, distinctive competencies, capabilities, competitive advantages, or resources that the organisation can draw on in selecting a strategy. Weaknesses are activities that the organisation does not do well or resources it needs but does not have. *Weaknesses* can be defined as the lack of one or more skills, distinctive competencies, competitive advantages, or resources.

It is important to note that our interest lies in the internal strengths or weaknesses of the organisation studied that are thus, in principle, likely to be strengthened or contested based on the managerial decisions taken by the organisation alone. We examine the strengths and weaknesses of the structure, the staff, the systems (of information and communication), the finances, and the partnerships from the resource point of view. We consider the present situation, but also the past (where do we come from?). We are also interested in external opportunities and threats facing the organisation: those that it cannot influence directly and easily, but that it can attempt to benefit from or must avoid. *Opportunities* are situations in which benefits are fairly clear and likely to be realised if certain actions are taken. *Threats* are situations that give rise to potentially harmful events and outcomes if action is not taken in the immediate future; they must be actively confronted to prevent trouble.

The micro-environment (consisting of partners, those providing funds, competitors, regulatory bodies, public authorities, stakeholders) is often distinguished from the macro-environment (political, social, cultural, and technological aspects). The size of the institution has no consequence in this type of analysis. Chelladurai (2001, p. 123) presents a SWOT analysis for a simple tennis club.

There is no particular order in which this internal and external analysis should be carried out. It is possible to begin with either the internal or the external aspects, although it is usually external factors that trigger awareness that a strategic analysis is necessary. In fact, the various factors emerge fairly rapidly once the brainstorming starts. It is simply worth listing and classifying them in a 2 × 2 matrix (see below).

Such a matrix can be produced quite easily but also in a very superficial way. To avoid this trap, several drafts can be produced through brainstorming and discussed until a final matrix is adopted. A strategic planning survey can be distributed beforehand and the responses received from stakeholders used as a first input in the process of establishing the SWOT matrix. Software for creating these matrices exists, for example, Smartt (www.smartt.co.za/swot). It is sometimes difficult at the outset to decide whether an external factor is an opportunity or a threat. It is always possible to position such a factor, provisionally, at the border of the corresponding fields. We should never forget that the Chinese word for "crisis" consists of the characters for "threat, danger" and "hidden opportunity." For instance, the International Olympic Committee crisis in 1999, which represented major threats to its very existence, provided the opportunity for the organisation to make major reforms.

Internal analysis can lead to shedding light on specific competencies of the organisation that distinguish it from other, similar ones. External analysis must lead to the identification of key factors for success (or targets) that are essential in order for the organisation's strategy to succeed. These factors and these competencies are the inputs for creating a strategy.

2.2 Vision, Mission, and Objectives (Step 2)

Internal and external analysis has made it possible to determine the potential (strategic) actions that target one or several SWOT factors. Those that address several factors are the most important.

It is now necessary to structure these actions by defining the vision, mission, and objectives that the organisation wishes to adopt. These terms are used in different ways by different authors, and we now explain the meaning we apply to them:

- Vision = (very) long-term goal (seemingly out of reach)

- Mission = the reason for the organisation to exist

- Objectives = what we want to (or can) achieve in practical but not too detailed terms

The notions of vision and mission are extremely close to each other and sometimes mistaken for each other. A vision refers to shared values that are implied and to an ideal that is difficult to attain and as such is often not expressed—for instance, "The vision of the World Anti-Doping Agency (WADA) is a world that values and fosters doping-free sport." The vision of the IAAF (International Association of Athletics Federations) is for athletics "to

	Internal analysis	External analysis
Optimistic view	Strengths 1._____ 2._____ 3._____ etc.	Opportunities 1._____ 2._____ 3._____ etc.
Pessimistic view	Weaknesses 1._____ 2._____ 3._____ etc.	Threats 1._____ 2._____ 3._____ etc.

2 × 2 matrix for internal and external analysis.

remain the number one sport for individuals in a changing world."

The mission is particularly important in nonprofit organisations, whose goal is not to share profits and that work to a large extent with volunteers and donors whom it must continue to motivate. The main mission of a company is to make profits in order to remunerate its shareholders or owners. The mission of a nonprofit organisation (whether sport or other) cannot be limited to this lucrative objective, since any funds raised must be used to fulfil a mission reputed to be nobler and more idealistic. As the CEO of a large company interviewed by Drucker says (Drucker 1989, p. 89), "The businesses I work with start their planning with financial returns. The nonprofits start with the performance of their mission." Some authors, such as Slack (1997, p. 103), propose defining the mission before proceeding to a SWOT analysis. It is, however, important to be very familiar with the internal and external context before (re)formulating a mission or, possibly, confirming an existing one.

A mission gives the "big idea" of your organisation. It should help share the organisation's "dream." Theoretically, a mission serves three purposes: pinpointing a sector of activities, motivating those providing funds/donors and the leaders and staff or other stakeholders, and helping to evaluate the success of the organisation.

The development of a mission statement should follow a discussion on shared values. The mission statement must be congruent with the desired organisational values. Four questions must be answered:

- Why does this sport organisation exist?
- What function does the organisation perform? What services does it offer?
- For whom does the organisation perform this (these) function(s)?
- How does the organisation fulfil this (these) function(s)?

Chelladurai (2001, p. 131) presents the missions of the Athletics and Recreation Departments of Ohio Sate University.

The following are some examples of the missions of Olympic sport organisations.

OLYMPIC MOVEMENT MISSION

(Adopted in 1990 as Olympic Charter Fundamental Principles 3 and 6)

The goal of Olympism is to place everywhere sport at the service of the harmonious development of man, with a view to encouraging the establishment of a peaceful society concerned with the preservation of human dignity . . . by educating youth through sport practised without discrimination of any kind and in the Olympic spirit, which requires mutual understanding with a spirit of friendship, solidarity and fair play.

UCI MISSION

(Adopted in 1994)

The mission of the International Cycling Union (UCI) is to develop and promote all aspects of cycling without discrimination of any kind, in close cooperation with National Federations and major associates. By all aspects of cycling we mean:

- Sport with its natural and universal values of competition, effort and character-building, well-being and fair-play;
- A healthy form of recreation as tourism and leisure;
- An economical (affordable), ecological and environmentally friendly means of transport that helps to solve the mobility problems of modern society.

FIVB MISSION

(Adopted in 1995)

The FIVB (Fédération Internationale de Volley-Ball) governs, manages and communicates all forms of Volleyball and Beach Volleyball worldwide. It aims to develop Volleyball as a major world media and entertainment sport through world class planning and organisation of competitions, marketing and promotional activities.

USOC VISION STATEMENT

(Adopted in June 1996)

The United States Olympic Committee is dedicated to preparing America's athletes to represent the United States in the ongoing pursuit and achievement of excellence in the Olympic Games and in life. Our Olympians inspire Americans, particularly our youth, to embrace Olympic ideals and to pursue excellence in sport and in their lives.

USOC MISSION

(Adopted in 2000 after a change of CEO)

Preserve and promote the Olympic ideal as an effective, positive role model that inspires all Americans.

To lead the world's best Olympic organization in enabling United States athletes to sustain the highest levels of competitive excellence, and through their achievements be a source of inspiration for the Olympic ideal. There is no single sporting event that is more captivating and unifying than the Olympic Games. The accomplishments of United States athletes engender great national pride. The character they exhibit in their pursuit of athletic excellence provides vivid testimony to the nobility of the human spirit.

USOC MISSION

(Adopted in 2002 after another change of CEO)

Lead the world's best National Olympic Committee: Help U.S. Olympic athletes achieve sustained competitive excellence while inspiring all Americans and preserving the Olympic ideal. The USOC shall fulfill its mission on a basis consistent with Section 220503 of the Ted Stevens Olympic and Amateur Sports Act (the "Act"), which sets for the purposes of the USOC. [Section 220503 of this U.S. law lists 14 purposes for USOC.]

ACOG (ATLANTA COMMITTEE FOR THE OLYMPIC GAMES) MISSION STATEMENT

(Adapted for the 1996 Games)

- To conduct the Centennial Olympic Games with sensitivity, integrity, fiscal responsibility, and commitment to the needs of athletes;
- To share with the world the spirit of America, the experience of the American South, and the vision of Atlanta;
- To leave a positive physical and spiritual legacy and an indelible mark on Olympic history by staging the most memorable Olympic Games ever.

ATHOC (ATHENS OLYMPIC COMMITTEE) VISION

In 2004, the Olympic Games are returning to their ancient birthplace and the city of their revival. Athletes from all nations will unite in Greece to engage in noble competition. The Athens Olympic Games will combine history, culture and peace, with sports and Olympism. The people of Greece shall host a unique Games on a human scale, inspiring the world to celebrate Olympic Values. [This statement is completed by nine objectives]

IAAF (INTERNATIONAL ASSOCIATION OF ATHLETICS FEDERATIONS) VISION FOR ATHLETICS

(Adopted in 2003)

To remain the number one sport for individuals in a changing world. The vision for the sport has been the guiding light in identifying what the sport should be doing. The mission statement, encompassing all the objectives set out in this [Athletics' World] plan, defines in more detail what the sport of Athletics aims to achieve. . . . To ensure that Athletics remains at the forefront of the world's sporting community and maintains its position as the ultimate embodiment of the spirit of sport by offering all people the greatest opportunities to participate at all levels, providing the greatest possible spectacle to the public and the media, thereby developing its long-term appeal and values.

GYMNASTICS CANADA

(National Federation or Governing Body)

To promote and provide positive and diverse gymnastics experiences through the delivery of comprehensive quality gymnastics programming by:

- Leading the Canadian gymnastics system
- Directing High Performance programs in the pursuit of international excellence
- Guiding the development of national programs at all levels

Gymnastics Canada sets the operating standards and practices for the sport in Canada, from coaching certification and athlete development, to judging certification programs and standards of ethical behaviour.

NATIONAL STRATEGY FOR SPORT 2003-2007

(Produced by SportScotland in 2003)

A vision for Scotland:

- A country where sport is more widely available to all.
- A country where sporting talent is recognised and nurtured.
- A country achieving and sustaining world-class performances in sport.

The visions or missions (or both) of most U.S. national sport governing bodies (NSFs) can be found in appendix B.

The words chosen for a mission are extremely important. The people drawing the mission up should not be afraid of being somewhat general and idealistic. However, the risk exists of becoming entrenched in how to define a mission without moving on to more concrete concerns. It is important to resist this tendency by defining precise objectives.

Objectives are a way to specify the mission in more detail. Objectives must be SMART (Significant, Measurable, Action oriented and Accepted, Realistic, Time related). In other words, they should not be too general; they must be achievable within a certain time period, and it must be possible to measure, quantitatively or qualitatively, whether they have been achieved. Here are some examples:

USOC STRATEGIC PLAN'S FOUR MAIN GOALS (1996)

- Continually improve the performance of U.S. athletes in international competitions.
- Become the most prestigious and respected sport organization in the U.S. (track 1), and increase the presence at the IOC and IF level in order to provide greater support to American athletes and sport entities (track 2).
- Build and strengthen USOC Brand(s).
- Enhance USOC's organizational governance.

SLOOC (SALT LAKE OLYMPIC ORGANIZING COMMITTEE) PRIMARY GOALS (2002)

SLOC has adopted five primary goals for the 2002 Olympic Winter Games:

- To carefully plan and execute excellent, fiscally responsible Games
- To creative positive experiences and memories for all participants in the Games
- To leave a legacy of facilities and opportunities for the athletes of the United States and the world, and for the children of Utah
- To introduce the spirit and optimism of Utah and the American West to the world
- To share a passion for the land chosen to stage the Games

SCOTLAND'S 11 TARGETS FOR 2007

(From Sport 21, The National Strategy for Sport 2003-2007)

By 2007

- 80% of primary schoolchildren will be physically active;
- we will have made progress towards all schoolchildren taking part in at least two hours of high quality physical education classes a week;
- 85% of those aged 13-17 will take part in sport, in addition to the school curriculum, more than once a week;
- 49% of those aged 14 plus in Social Inclusion Partnership areas will take part in sport at least once a week;
- 55% of those aged 17-24 will take part in sport more than twice a week;
- 43% of those aged 45-64 will take part in sport at least once a week;
- over 250 Scots will have been medallists on the world stage;
- Scotland will have over 500 sports halls available to the public so that 70% of Scots have access to a hall within 20 minutes walk;
- over one million Scots will play sport in membership of clubs;
- Scotland will sustain 150,000 volunteers who are contributing to the development and delivery of Scottish sport;
- every local authority area's community planning process will have contributed to the targets of Sport 21 2003-2007.

IAAF OBJECTIVES FOR THE SPORT OF ATHLETICS

(Adopted in 2003)

At the centre of the plan is the Event Objective which aims to improve the staging of events at all levels within the sport. Supporting this are the Objectives aimed at building the sport internally and selling the sport externally. The following Objectives therefore ensure that the requirements of all constituent groups are considered.

Event Objective

- To improve the quality and appeal of Athletics events.

Participation Objectives

- To provide all people with the greatest opportunities to participate in Athletics.

- To make Athletics the worldwide number one participatory sport in schools.

Tools Objectives

- To increase the level of competence in the sport of Athletics.
- To improve access to Athletics facilities and equipment for all.

Public Objective

- To increase the recognition of the sport of Athletics.

Media Objective

- To increase the quality and quantity of media coverage of Athletics.

Partners Objective

- To ensure the long term financial security of the sport of Athletics.

Each objective is further detailed with several focus areas and actions within each focus area.

At times, one encounters the words "goals" or "policies" or "targets" rather than "objectives." Objectives can be ordered from the most general to the most detailed, but avoiding too many levels (two or three maximum) is recommended. It is necessary to analyse the feasibility of the objectives and their potential risks before retaining them definitively.

2.3 Strategy and Tactics (Step 3)

Strategy must map out how to reach the objectives. Strategy must coordinate tactics. Tactics are concrete actions for key (strategic) areas. They provide replies to the questions Who? When? How? How much? They deal with the use of resources. Tactics are sometimes called activities (cf. WADA's Strategic Plan) or actions (cf. IAAF's Athletics' World Plan). These are the activities/actions that (operational) management must carry out.

"A wide consensus now exists that strategic management should be considered as the ongoing organiser of the necessary alignment between the requirements of the environment and the capacities of the enterprise" (Martinet 1984, p. 1).

Strategy and tactics must take into account financial, human, and information resources available as well as the resources that would be ideal in order to achieve the objectives. They are often accompanied by a budget dealing with money and time, which can evolve according to how the strategy and tactics are applied. The strategic plans for the Canadian Olympic Committee and for some national federations in that country are appended to this document (see appendix A).

A strategic plan should be about 10 to 30 pages and should be a mixture of text, charts, tables, and bullet points. It should focus on communicating key messages. The authors should allow time to get the wording right. The plan must be distributed throughout the organisation and not kept confidential. It should also be made available to all stakeholders, for example through a Web site or well-designed brochures.

Here are some common pitfalls in establishing a strategic plan:

- Too much paperwork
- Insufficient emphasis on identifying key issues, opportunities, and threats
- Lack of integration of services and fundraising
- No measure of performance
- No implementation timetable
- No allocation of responsibilities
- Agreement to the plan but insufficient personal commitment to make it happen, especially from governing body and chief executive

In a rare work focused on voluntary sport organisations, Thibault et al. (1993) identified six strategic imperatives to be considered when developing strategies (and tactics):

- Fundability: the ability of the sport organisation to secure financial resources from external sources
- Size of client base: the number of clients the sport organisation serves
- Volunteer appeal: the organisation's ability to attract human resources
- Support group appeal: the extent to which the sport organisation's programs are visible and appealing to those groups capable of providing current or future support

- Equipment cost: the amount of money required for equipment at the introductory levels of the sport
- Affiliation fees: the costs associated with participating in a sport (Slack 1997, p. 109)

Although developed and tested only for Canadian sport organisations (national governing bodies), these imperatives can most certainly be considered for sport organisations in other countries and at other levels when choosing strategies. It should be noted that the first four imperatives qualify the attractiveness of the sport organisation's programmes for its current clients, while the last two qualify its competitive position regarding clients/potential members. These two dimensions can be crossed within a matrix in order to pinpoint various types of strategy (Thibault et al. 1993).

The combination of analysis, the vision/mission, objectives, strategy, and tactics constitutes what could be called a strategic plan. (The internal and external SWOT analysis is also frequently appended to this.) We can even define strategic management, like Peters, as the application of a (strategic) plan: "The management of an organization according to an explicit strategic plan is strategic management. It involves the execution of an explicit strategic plan that has captured the commitment of the people who must execute it; that is consistent with the values, beliefs, and culture of those people; and for which they have the required competence to execute" (Peters 1984, p. 111).

The following stages can be followed to involve all those concerned:

- Governing body and senior management agree on process.
- Management prepares strategic review statement.
- Stakeholders are consulted on key issues from review.
- Management prepares draft strategic plan.
- Trustees and other stakeholders are consulted on draft.

- Governing body considers and agrees on plan.
- Management links with budgets.
- Management communicates throughout the organisation.
- Trustees and management monitor implementation.

For carrying out genuine strategic management, this plan should not remain locked away in a drawer. It must inspire operational and daily management, which allocates the human, financial, and information resources. There is a need for a periodic shift in emphasis from what to how and back again, which creates a "dance of the what and how" (Nutt and Backoff 1992, p. 417), in which the managers' intuition and creativity are essential.

This results in an intended strategy that must, in line with the idea by Mintzberg (1994, p. 24), be combined with an emergent strategy that comes out of the developments and constraints of daily activities in order to create the strategy that is genuinely achieved (see figure 1.1). Then it must be evaluated in the light of intentions. This is the last stage of this simplified process.

2.4 Benchmarks and Indicators (Step 4)

Strategic management requires an ongoing evaluation. This is best achieved through measurable indicators and benchmarks that have been set with the objectives attached to the mission at step 2. These indicators should be SPORTS (Specific, Pertinent, Objective, Representative, Transparent, Simple).

Such an evaluation should also be used to improve future strategic planning and reassess the internal and external situation of the organisation, thereby closing the loop. This is when strategic management merges into performance management (see part II).

References to strategic plans in Olympic sport organisations are given in appendix B.

three

The Olympic System and the New Actors in World Sport

Any strategic analysis requires a sound knowledge of the context or the environment within which the given organisations evolve. The acronym SWOT (see previous chapter) also has a French version, EMOFF (Environnement, Menaces, Opportunités, Forces, Faiblesses), which includes environment as an additional term. Here, studying the environment in which the given organisation operates precedes the process and serves to better identify the threats and opportunities that the organisation encounters, as well as its strengths and weaknesses.

Nonprofit sport organisations are linked to what can be called the Olympic system (Chappelet 1991), a pyramidal unit of organisations, shown in the next section, and one that contains everything from basic sport practice (clubs) to the elite level (Olympic Games). For about 20 years, however, other organisations—and often those based on profit—have shown an interest in this system because sport has become an industry, that is, an economic sector in its own right. It is important to discover these new organisations in order to gain a better understanding of the environment of sport organi-

sations, which are for the most part nonprofit ones. This is what we discuss in the second part of this chapter.

3.1 The Olympic System

Entities that contribute toward the preparation and running of the Olympic Games (or Olympic sport organisations, OSOs) can be broken down into five major types of actors that maintain close relations, making this a well-structured system, also known under the wider term the "Olympic Movement."[1]

The International Olympic Committee (IOC), founded in 1894, constitutes the leading actor at the summit of the system because it recognises the other actors of the Olympic Movement and partially finances them. Although its role has expanded progressively to almost all aspects of sport, it remains strongly focused on the Olympic Games, for which it possesses all legal rights thanks to the worldwide registration of numerous marks associated with it (symbol, flag, flame, motto, etc.). These rights generate considerable revenues that the IOC shares with

---

[1]The International Olympic Committee includes legal persons and individuals (athletes, coaches, sport officials, etc.) within the Olympic Movement who accept being guided by the Olympic Charter that it has drawn up (principle 5). However, it recognises only legal persons (Article 4 of the Olympic Charter). Its main stated role is to lead the promotion of Olympism (Article 2).

the other actors. The International Paralympic Committee (IPC) is the equivalent of the IOC for the Paralympic Games, which, since 1988, follow on from the Olympic Games in the same city. The headquarters of the IOC are in Lausanne, Switzerland, and those of the IPC are in Bonn, Germany.

The Organising Committees for the Olympic Games (OCOGs)—like the ACOG or SLOOC (refer to chapter 2, section 2.2)—are a second type of actor. Although temporary, since their life span does not exceed about 10 years (including the candidature and closure phases), they are at the centre of the Olympic system and permit the system to finance itself thanks to the revenues obtained from the Winter or Summer Games. An OCOG usually maintains close relations with the local, regional, and national public authorities of a country for numerous organisational questions (construction, security, transport, diplomatic issues, etc.). Today, OCOGs concentrate on the preparation and the organisation as such of the Games, while parallel organisations are devoted to tasks close to the public authorities such as the construction of facilities, security, or transport.

The international sport federations (IFs)— such as the FIVB, the UCI, or the IAAF (refer to chapter 2, section 2.2)—constitute a third type of actor. They govern their sport on a worldwide level (rules, competitions, sanctions, etc.). They are divided up between those (35 in 2004) whose sport is on the programme of the Summer or Winter Games, which sanctions their Olympic events, and those (30) whose sport is not included on the programme but is recognised by the IOC. The Olympic federations receive a portion of television broadcasting rights for the Games. Recognised IFs receive subsidies. Since 1967, the Olympic and recognised IFs have come together with other IFs to form the General Association of International Sports Federations (GAISF), whose headquarters are in Monaco. The IFs' activities are by no means restricted to the Games. A very few IFs, such as the FIFA (Fédération Internationale de Football Association) have World Championships whose size rivals that of the Games.

The national Olympic committees (NOCs)— such as USOC (refer to chapter 2, section 2.2)—form a fourth type of actor within the Olympic system. They are the territorial representatives (202 in 2004) of the IOC, and they alone are allowed to submit an Olympic team to the Games. They receive forms of aid from the IOC via Olympic Solidarity (OS), an organisation based in Lausanne and financed to an extent—approximately one-third—by television broadcasting rights for the Games. The NOCs are often subsidised by their governments and are sometimes (para-) governmental organisations. To an ever-increasing extent, they also constitute the confederation of national sport federations (the main European exceptions here are Germany, Ireland, and the United Kingdom). Since 1980, the NOCs have come together to form a (world) association of NOCs (ANOC), headquartered in Paris, that acts as the parent organisation to five continental associations that share the funds from Olympic Solidarity. Three of these are responsible for holding Continental Games (Pan American, Asian, African).

The national sport federations (NSFs)—such as Gymnastics Canada (refer to chapter 2, section 2.2)—are the fifth and final type of actor within the Olympic system. They associate, for a given sport, the clubs and regional associations in their countries and, via these, their athletes. The NSFs can be recognised at a national level by the NOC of their country or, at an international level, by the IF for their sport (or by both). At times this double recognition is not obtained, preventing the participation of these athletes at the Games.

These five types of actors can be represented in the form of five rings, but with a layout that is different from that of the Olympic rings (see figure 3.1). The Olympic Charter drawn up by the IOC is their founder text, and the athletes are their main reason for existence.

Virtually all the organisations within the Olympic system are nonprofit ones according to the law of the country where their headquarters are located, including the IOC in Switzerland. For about 20 years, this associative movement has been increasingly confronted with four other types of actor whose legal nature is different, as described in the next section.

3.2 The New Actors in World Sport

Porter (1980) proposed a famous diagram to analyse the various facets of an industry.

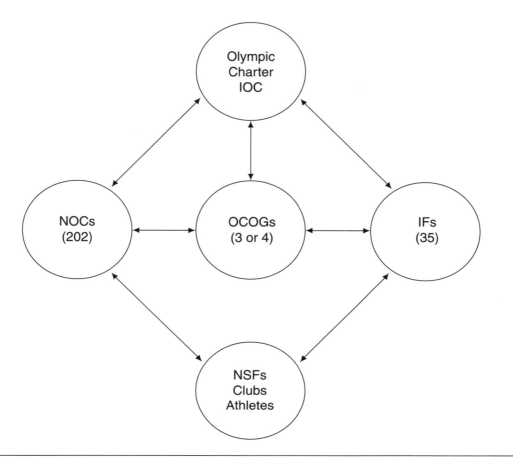

Figure 3.1 The Olympic system.

Oster (1995, p. 30) adapted this to analyse the environment of the nonprofit organisation and to provide a better view of the pressures that come to bear on organisations that are already implanted within a field of action (see figure 3.2).

In turn, we can transpose this diagram for the sport industry (see figure 3.3). The diagram

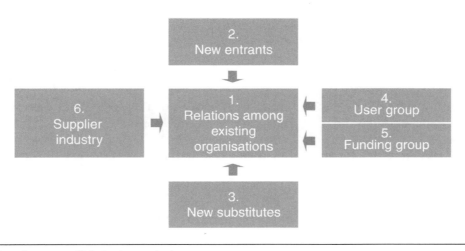

Figure 3.2 Chart for nonprofit industry analysis.

From STRATEGIC MANAGEMENT OF NONPROFIT ORGANIZATIONS by S.M. Oster, copyright 1995 by Oxford University Press. Used by permission of Oxford University Press, Inc.

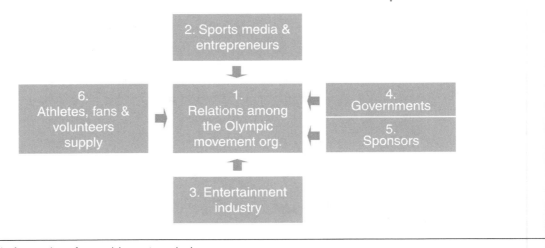

Figure 3.3 Six-force chart for world sport analysis.

allows us to gain a better grasp of the new actors in world sport.

First come governments and intergovernmental organisations, public law entities that are becoming increasingly interested in sport because it has become a socioeconomic phenomenon that affects an extremely large sector of the population. Governments also finance sport at the local, regional, and national levels. Examples of such organisations include SportScotland (refer to chapter 2, section 2.2) and the Irish Sports Council (refer to chapter 4, section 4.5). As a result of particular legal situations or cases of unfavourable developments such as doping, violence, and corruption linked to sport, States and organisations such as the Council of Europe and the European Union have begun to pay strong attention to sport and the Olympic system. For example, the World Anti-Doping Agency was created as a result of strong pressures from governments on the Olympic Movement.

A second new type of actor is multinational companies that provide international sponsoring and maintain a commercial relationship with the IOC and the IFs or their continental equivalents. These include, for example, the dozen companies that participate in the IOC's TOP (The Olympic Partners) marketing programme (Coca-Cola, Kodak, Visa, McDonald's, etc.). The headquarters of these multinationals are often in the United States.

Their equivalents on a national level (sponsors and the national media) are a third type of new actor and have relations with the NOCs and NSFs via sponsoring contracts limited to their national territory. For example, in Switzerland, the soft drink manufacturer Rivella has for many years supported the Swiss Olympic Association (NOC of Switzerland) and several of the country's sport federations that are members of this latter group.

Television networks (such as NBC [National Broadcasting Corporation], the channels belonging to the European Broadcasting Union) pay considerable rights to the IOC in order to broadcast the Olympic Games. As such, they can be considered genuine sponsors but remain (with very few exceptions) restricted to their national territory. They are, moreover, the most essential sponsors for attracting others. National and international sponsors are usually limited stock companies.

Finally, a fourth type of actor has been emerging strongly for approximately the last 10 years, in cooperation with or competing against the NSFs and the IFs. These are leagues of teams or professional athletes. This category includes groups of athletes such as Association of Tennis Professionals (ATP), Women's Tennis Association (WTA), Professional Golf Association (PGA), and Association of Surfing Professionals (ASP). It also includes professional football leagues or leagues of other team sports found in most European countries or those that major clubs are attempting to create (G14-18 in football, ULEB in basketball), as well as professional American leagues such as National Basketball Association (NBA), National Hockey League (NHL), National (American) Football League

(NFL), and Major League Baseball (MLB). Although these new actors and their legal status vary widely, they have a common objective: achieving profit for their members, owners, or shareholders. At times, they cooperate with the Olympic system regarding the participation of their actors in the Games (the basketball Dream Team in Barcelona, NHL players in Nagano and Salt Lake City, etc.)

The position of these four new types of actor at the borders of the Olympic system and the ways in which they interact are shown in figure 3.4.

These new actors, like the macro-environment within which sport operates nowadays, constitute an equal number of good reasons for sport organisations within the Olympic system to carry out serious strategic approaches.

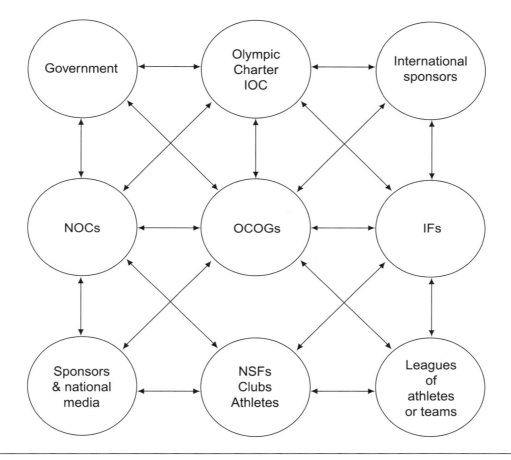

Figure 3.4 The new actors encircling the Olympic system.

four

Cases of Strategic Approaches by Some Olympic Sport Organisations

In this chapter we briefly present some strategic approaches in nonprofit sport organisations: two international federations (IFs) (volleyball and hockey), two worldwide organisations with sectorial responsibilities (paralympic sport and anti-doping), a national organisation (Ireland), two national Olympic committees (Zimbabwe and Malaysia), and a department within the IOC (Olympic Solidarity). These approaches illustrate the considerations discussed in chapters 1 and 2. They were often triggered by an evolution in the environment as described in chapter 3. For more details, readers may refer to information available on the Internet sites indicated. These strategic documents themselves are in fact not always easy to obtain since they reveal a great deal about the organisations from which they come.

4.1 International Volleyball Federation (FIVB)

The FIVB (Fédération Internationale de Volley-Ball) was no doubt one of the first IFs to take a strategic approach in order to inspire its management. The decision to do so came from its congress (assembly of national volleyball federations) at the time of the Olympic Games in Barcelona in 1992. A study commission was carefully set up for this purpose, to include representatives from all sectors of volleyball throughout the world. The commission met for the first time in January 1993, when it established its working principles, and held three successive meetings. In January 1994 the commission concluded its work for presentation to the FIVB Board of Administration. The FIVB Secretariat, under instructions from the FIVB's president, polished up the conclusions and programmes, giving the final format to the text of a document titled "Volleyball World Plan 2001." Its goal was to counter administrative and managerial shortcomings in most of the national volleyball federations and turn volleyball and beach volleyball into major sports at a world, continental, and national level by the year 2001. A total of 140 national federations grouped into five categories participated in this World Plan 2001.

After presenting an overview of the 1990s sport social environment, the plan analysed the internal problems of national volleyball federations and confederations and the external problems arising from today's international sport environment. It concluded with a number of policies to follow for the national federations and the FIVB itself, summarising these policies in five goals:

1. To make volleyball and beach volleyball MAJOR SPORTS at a world, continental, and national level.
2. To bring volleyball and beach volleyball on the front line on the international sport scene as TOP SPORTS FOR SPECTATORS, supported by the media.
3. To transform the most important national, continental and world beach volleyball and volleyball competitions into MEDIA EVENTS, heavily televised and duly financed by international sponsors.
4. To make each National Federation, Confederation and the FIVB itself, in the short term, the most professional organisations, each one at its own level, with modern, flexible, and efficient management.
5. To enlarge the number of countries able to play at the TOP LEVEL so as to present a more competitive, spectacular and attractive volleyball.

These goals were translated into specific programmes to be implemented at all levels by each of the members and institutions embodying the FIVB. These programmes, which create a "dance of the what and how" (and when), constitute the plan itself and are regrouped and structured for a better understanding of the tasks to be accomplished by each of the institutions concerned:

The FIVB and Its Confederations

- To unify the international structure of volleyball and beach volleyball
- To strengthen the authority of volleyball institutions
- To establish order in national and international competitions
- To raise the competitiveness of national teams of medium-level countries
- To make volleyball and beach volleyball more spectacular for TV and spectators

The National Federations

- To improve their administrative and management conditions

- To structure and operate national junior and youth programmes
- To structure a National Beach Volleyball Council and operate a National Beach Volleyball Circuit
- To prepare long-term planning of activities
- To improve local conditions for volleyball activities
- To propel volleyball's image as a TOP COMPETITION SPORT in their country

All Volleyball Institutions

- To properly implement the "Volleyball World Plan 2001"
- To make the World Plan 2001 work

The implementation of the plan was facilitated by management seminars and plan workshops in 1996 through 2000. Certain national federations launched their own approaches. The Swiss federation's approach has the title "Projet 2003." An award for the most outstanding national implementation of the world plan was given at the 2002 World Congress. To mention just a few benchmarks, in 2002, the FIVB had 218 national sport federations (NSFs) (200 in 1992), 33 million licensed athletes, and 500 million players; it awards over USD 25 million in prize money every year. Beach volleyball became an Olympic discipline in 1996. The professional circuit run by the Association of (Beach) Volleyball Professionals until 1999 is now under FIVB leadership. The FIVB claims to be one of the top three IFs and presents itself as the worldwide leader in innovative "new generation" sport entertainment. The FIVB President during this growth period has summarized his management experience in a recent book (Acosta 2002).

Following the completion of the World Plan 2001, the FIVB Board of Administration evaluated its positive results and shortcomings and named a steering committee to discuss and establish a new vision for volleyball for the ensuing years up to 2008. The Volleyball World Vision 2008 was adopted at the FIVB 2002 Congress in Buenos Aires. The main goal to be pursued in this vision is "to make each National Federation and Confederation the most professional organisations in short term, each one at its own level, with modern, flexible and efficient administration under professional management." The Vision 2008 report provides checklists for national federations as well as continental confederations to conduct their own SWOT analysis. It concludes with the overall and specific goals that the FIVB sets itself and the strategic actions to be undertaken in four areas: written press, radio and television, national and international competitions, and fundamental managerial principles.

More information related to this approach can be found at www.fivb.org.

4.2 International Hockey Federation (FIH)

The FIH (Fédération Internationale de Hockey) finalised its strategic plan in November 2000, following a highly successful Olympic tournament at the Sydney Olympic Games. Founded in 1908, the FIH felt the need to trace "the path ahead for the early part of the twenty-first century" (with 2005 as the first time target). This work was carried out by a commission with the help of consultants and on the basis of a SWOT analysis.

The strategic plan begins in a classical way by a reformulation of the FIH's mission:

The International Hockey Federation (FIH) is the world governing body for hockey. Our primary objective is to encourage, promote, develop and administer hockey at all levels in order to maximise participation, standards, enjoyment and community involvement. We achieve this by working collaboratively with all Member Associations, Continental Federations, government bodies, commercial enterprises and the media to realise our shared goals.

This mission is explained further with the help of a vision—"Our picture of the future":

The International Hockey Federation develops the vision for the growth of hockey and its aspirations for continued and increased success in the international sports world. Its success in the future will be visible by:

- Acknowledging the players at all levels as the cornerstone of FIH activities by consulting them and pursuing initiatives to achieve optimum conditions
- Promoting gender equality and accessibility for all people in the FIH and Continental Fed-

erations demonstrating leadership in world-level hockey matters

- Demonstrating leadership in world-level hockey matters
- Respecting the autonomous role of its member National Associations to deal with their local issues
- Providing assistance to members to achieve their uniquely developed goals within the FIH structure
- Working collaboratively with the Continental Federations to promote and develop hockey in their respective parts of the world
- Providing a cohesive, organisational framework for the global development of hockey
- Providing human and financial resources to develop all aspects of the sport
- Organising major and international events for hockey
- Increasing the number of nations competing in continental and global events
- Inspiring commitment and dedication for the success of hockey from its members
- Participating in the international world of sport at all appropriate administrative levels

This vision is supported by clearly expressed values:

- The well being of our athletes
- A positive, gender inclusive image
- Fair play, safety and integrity
- The Olympic movement and its ideals
- A consultative, creative approach to the development of hockey
- A worldwide and future development focus
- An efficient and effective administration

On the basis of a SWOT analysis, a number of "strategic priorities" are proposed for FIH:

- Make hockey an affordable sport for as much of the population as possible with the aim of increased participation and popularity
- Increase the number of competitors motivated to play high levels of hockey
- Establish FIH as a leading and efficient service provider to all affiliates, participants and to the Continental Federations
- Develop the game of indoor and outdoor hockey both on and off the field. Changes to

the rules, tournament structure, equipment, field of play, umpiring and on-field presentations will be made to both retain and increase the sport's appeal to play and watch in a fast-paced, continually changing world

- Improve the consistent quality and accessibility of coaching and umpiring services throughout the world
- Embrace modern technology to develop and enhance the game
- Maximise the marketing, merchandising and promotional opportunities associated with hockey to attract funds and sponsorships
- Make hockey more television friendly following a comprehensive study of the needs of broadcasters and television audiences
- Raise the FIH image through increased promotion of its activities to Member Associations, Continental Federations, National Olympic Committees, the International Olympic Committee and the media
- Increase the number of registered players in all categories
- Ensure a high level of participant safety and well-being
- Encourage the development of first class facilities and the installation of synthetic pitches throughout the world
- Strengthen hockey as an Olympic sport by understanding the special significance of Olympic participation for athletes and strengthen links with the IOC and AGFIS
- Review and continually improve the organisational structure of the FIH based on the principles of democracy, practical considerations, optimal communication and professional management

- Develop and promote Indoor Hockey on a worldwide basis to achieve a global competition format and/or active membership in a multi sport event organisation
- Develop and promote hockey for athletes with a disability
- Maintain and ensure the favourable gender balance, which exists in the playing, leadership and administration of hockey.

These priorities are summarised under eight "key result areas"—"that we must succeed at to achieve our mission": The player; Events; Umpiring; Equipment; Medical; Development and Coaching; Marketing and Communication; Operations and Finance.

For each key result area, a one-page document summarises the goals/objectives to be achieved through an action plan (with additional funding specified for each activity) and the performance indicators for each. For instance, the following is the document for the Events key result area:

This strategic plan is currently being applied. It is encouraging to see that national hockey federations such as that of Malta (Hockey Association of Malta) have also drawn up (strategic) plans at their level for developing this sport.

More information related to this approach can be found at www.fihockey.org.

4.3 International Paralympic Committee (IPC)

Although the IPC is well known for supervising and managing the Paralympic Games, which are now held two weeks after the Winter and Summer Games and in the same facilities, the

Goals	Objectives	Action plan	Indicators
To attract increased interest and expansion in world-level events via professional marketing and presentation strategies	• To develop and implement a major events marketing and presentation strategy • To ensure that world-level events and data are covered widely in all media	• Indoor World Cup every four years (USD TBA) • Youth Hockey Festival (USD 60,000) • Special projects (USD 4,000)	• Number of spectators at events and on TV • Number of inclusion of hockey in multisport events • Consistency in presentation of events • Introduction of prize money

committee felt in 2000 that it needed strategic planning to face its major concerns and challenges. These challenges arise since paralympic sport (i.e., sport for athletes with a disability) is growing rapidly, bringing new duties and new approaches regarding the setup of the organisation. For instance, today the IPC has more than 150 national members. At the time of its foundation in 1990, there were only 50 national Paralympic committees. The number of elite athletes has also increased dramatically, with the level of sport performance constantly rising.

In order to start its strategic process, the IPC convened a "Strategic Planning Congress" in Kuala Lumpur, Malaysia, over a full week in April 2001. About 250 delegates from 75 nations attended. The three main themes of the congress were future governance, roles and responsibilities, as well as structure of the IPC. These themes were summarised by the IPC President in his opening address:

- Whether or not we should be responsible only for the Paralympic Games
- Whether or not we should reexamine the roles and responsibilities of our elected officials now that we have professional staff
- Whether or not we should change the size, scope, role, and responsibility of our EC, MC, IOSDs, GAs, Regional Committees, and Sport Committees.

Through teamwork ("breakout discussions") among the delegates, facilitated by consultants, each of these themes produced key concerns, consensus statements, and recommendations for the IPC board and management.

The IPC vision, mission, and core values were determined as follows:

The Vision of the International Paralympic Committee (IPC) is to be indisputably recognized as one of the most successful and influential Sport Organizations in the world; to gain international respect and reputation as a major advocate for the promotion of the rights, recognition and equality of athletes with a disability throughout the world; and, to meet the needs of those athletes as they pursue and achieve excellence in sport.

The Mission of the International Paralympic Committee (IPC) is to serve our worldwide community of athletes with a disability though the creation, development and promotion of sport opportunities. The Mission to be served through participation at Paralympic Games, multidisability World and Regional Championships, and through the provision of administrative support services including but not limited to marketing strategies, development, communication networks and the like.

Core Values

- Sport for all
- Democratic, open & participative organization
- Athletes-centred
- Teamwork & leadership integrity
- Respect and Trust
- Quality of life

The strategic plan was organised around immediate follow-up actions, short-term actions (before or in 2003), and medium-/long-term actions (2004, 2005 or beyond):

Immediate

- Congress report/Summary of recommendations to all members of IPC: Response questionnaire for recommendations.
- IPC Peer Evaluation—all functional units (satisfaction, areas of strengths/weaknesses, prioritization of tasks, areas for improvement, self-evaluation).
- Communication strategy and plan (improve speed, improve access, transparency & accountability, feedback/interaction).
- Review handbook (identify sections/clauses requiring change, e.g., IOSDs (International Organisations of Sport for the Disabled), sports, IPC-IOC relationship, Executive Committee/positions).
- Candidates for election 2001 to submit quadrennial plan.

Short-Term

- Executive Committee 2001-2005 (consolidate a quadrennial plan first quarter 2002, create a strategic service structure: e.g. commission, department, or consultancy, research unit).

- Prepare IPC Charter Strategic Plan for General Assembly 2003 (athlete-centred, all functions: sports, regions, IOSDs, external policy: IOC, IFs-GAISF, etc., financial plan and strategy).
- Proposals for overall change in constitution, structure, partnership agreements for approval of General Assembly 2003.

Long-Term

- Evolution of specific sports, regions, IOSDs.

In 2003, the IPC adopted a new corporate identity centred on its new strategy. It included a new logo and motto ("Spirit in Motion"). Its vision was simplified as follows: "To enable paralympic athletes to achieve sporting excellence and inspire and excite the world." A corporate brochure presents this vision and outlines the IPC's identity ("Who we are"), focus ("What we do"), history ("Where we are from"), and direction ("Where we are going"). This brochure constitutes a good example of what many sport organisations should do to communicate their strategy to their constituency and the outside world.

Documents related to this approach, which is at the initial stages, can be found at www.paralympic.org.

4.4 World Anti-Doping Agency (WADA)

The WADA was founded in November 1999 following the World Conference on Doping organised in Lausanne by the IOC and attended by many governmental representatives. It has the particularity of uniting, in equal proportions, representatives of the Olympic Movement and public authorities among its executive bodies (Chappelet 2002).

A strategic plan was developed by WADA from its foundation to more clearly focus its activities and resources over the following two to five years. Such a plan was requested by public authorities for confirmation of the funding of their half of WADA's budget. This plan was finalised in July 2001 and approved by a subsequent WADA Board. The approach was carried out by consultants. The plan begins by listing, without specific justification, the vision, the mission, and the eight goals of WADA:

The vision of WADA is a world that values and fosters doping-free sport.

The mission of WADA is to promote and coordinate, on an international basis, the fight against doping in sport in all its forms.

Goals

1. To be an independent organisation that follows and leads in the development of best practices in its administration, finance, and general operations to ensure the success of its mandate.
2. To be an organisation recognised as an anti-doping leader on behalf of sport and athletes.
3. To have a universal Anti-Doping Code covering all sports and countries.
4. To have internationally harmonised rules and regulations governing the operation of national anti-doping programs.
5. To co-ordinate a world wide program for in- and out-of-competition testing.
6. To develop anti-doping education and prevention programs at the international level aimed at promoting the practice of doping-free sport according to ethical principles.
7. To establish and manage targeted research programs relating to detection of doping and protection of athletes' health.
8. To establish and implement a laboratory accreditation program.

For each of the eight goals, lengthy tables specify the strategies and programme activities that must be put in place (these latter for the short, medium, or long term) plus performance benchmarks to be controlled according to this planning. For example, the eighth goal (to establish and implement a laboratory accreditation system) is illustrated in the figure on page 29.

This strategic planning is completed by a financial plan that defines the sources of revenues (Olympic Movement, public authorities, sponsors, grants, etc.) envisaged until 2005, the target date for the plan to be completed. However, there is no precise allocation of revenues between strategies and programme activities. In November 2002, the plan was revised to include three more goals concerning effective communication and government relations strategies, as well as a Global Clearing House to assist in

Strategies	Program activities	Performance benchmarks
Establish an international network of accredited laboratories and standards of performance and expertise and continuous quality control	Short term (2001): Establish a Laboratory Accreditation Subcommittee to advance the development of a WADA accreditation system	Committee established, meetings occurred, framework agreed upon
	Medium term (2002): Develop a Laboratory Accreditation and Quality Control Program that includes interlaboratory comparability and continuous quality control assessment	System established, endorsed by WADA Board
	Longer term (2003-2005): Conclude transition agreement regarding accreditation of laboratories so that accreditation is by WADA	WADA recognised as the authority for laboratory accreditation
	Complete the Laboratory Accreditation System, etc.	Number of laboratories accredited, etc.

the implementation of an open and transparent doping control program.

It is interesting that the structural organisation chart of the WADA administration in 2002 was to a large extent drawn from this strategic plan. In fact, each strategic goal corresponds more or less to an operational directorate under a director general who reports to the board. There is perhaps no better way of following the precept "Structure follows strategy" advanced by Chandler as early as 1962, even if this is easier in a new organisation where the structures already in place are not so cumbersome that they often determine strategy, as Peters pointed out (1984).

At the end of 2003, WADA fully revised its strategy and adopted a new Strategic Plan for 2004 through 2009 following consultations and input from its partners, the Olympic Movement and public authorities. The plan confirms WADA's vision and mission. It provides for the first time a set of the agency's core values: independence, ethical approach, accountability, professionalism, best practice, and innovation.

In its efforts, and as outlined in its Strategic Plan, the Agency now concentrates on five strategic objectives:

- To implement, support, oversee and monitor compliance of the World Anti-Doping Code.

- To educate and inform signatories to the Code, Governments and athletes/support personnel about the dangers and consequence of doping abuse.
- To lead, coordinate and support effective world class Anti-Doping Research Programmes.
- To increase the capability of Anti-Doping Organizations (ADOs) to implement anti-doping rules and programs to ensure compliance with the Code.
- To achieve the financial viability and resources to enable WADA to implement its Strategic Plan.

Each objective is completed by the desired outcome and the strategic actions required to achieve this outcome.

More information and the documents relating to this approach can be found at www.wada-ama.org (section: About WADA; sub-section: Strategic Plan).

4.5 Irish Sports Council (ISC)

The ISC was established in July 1999 to a high degree of expectation among Irish sport bodies in general. Its mission is to plan, lead, and coordinate the sustainable development of sport in Ireland. The ISC was immediately challenged to spell out its strategy to the Minister of

Tourism and Sport and, in turn, to the sporting public. This was achieved through consultation with the ISC partners, colleagues in relevant government departments, local authorities, and the public. The strategy builds on work undertaken previously to assess the global sport environment and the key challenges facing Irish sport.

The final document is titled, rather pompously, "A New Era for Sport: The ISC's Strategy 2000-2002." It begins with a single page of highlights that summarises the ISC's vision, priorities, and underpinnings:

Our Vision. We want Ireland to be a country in which:

- Everyone is welcomed and valued in sport, irrespective of their ability and background
- Individuals can enjoy developing their sporting abilities to the maximum of their talent
- Irish sportsmen and women achieve consistent world class performance, fairly

Our Priorities:

- Working in partnership with NGBs to make them more effective in developing their sport and servicing the needs of their members
- Influencing all those national programmes and initiatives which directly or indirectly impact on sport
- Fostering and supporting innovative Local Sports Partnerships at County or City level, designed to co-ordinate and promote the development of sport, particularly in disadvantaged areas. Promoting the appointment of at least one Sports Officer in each Local Sports Partnership
- Working with Local Sports partnerships and National Governing Bodies of Sport (NGBs), as appropriate, to promote participation and develop sporting potential

- Developing the holistic system of support services our leading sportsmen and women need to achieve world-class success.

Underpinned by:

- Fair play
- Effective, fact-based decision making
- Increased state and corporate support for sport
- All-island planning.

Following a discussion on ISC's core values and legal mandate, the document spells out three strategies (areas of intervention):

- Participatory strategy—to break down barriers and increase participation in sport, not only the number of people but their continued participation throughout their lives.
- Performance strategy—to create an environment so that individuals can develop their sporting abilities.
- Excellence strategy—to help our leading sportsmen and women achieve world-class success by fair and ethical means.

For each strategy, "key strategic initiatives" are determined for the next three years. These initiatives are distributed among four "delivery teams," that is, units of the ISC staff. This helps in measuring the quantitative and qualitative performance of each team and, globally, of the ISC. For instance, in 2000, for the Fair Play Team, which is to work in concert with everybody in sport to implement and promote all aspects of fair play, the initiatives are illustrated in the figure below.

The strategy of the ISC concludes with an examination of the financial resources made available by the State and by the distribution mechanisms to the different partners within Irish sport. More information and most

Removing barriers and increasing participation	Developing ability	Achieving world class success
• Code of Ethics launch • Code of Ethics marketing and awareness campaign • Coordination of leadership training	• Code of Ethics marketing and awareness campaign • Anti-doping education and testing programme	• Anti-doping education a testing programme • Research

of the documents relating to this approach can be found at www.irishsportscouncil.ie/strategy.asp.

4.6 Zimbabwe Olympic Committee (ZOC)

In 2000 and 2001, the ZOC President followed the MEMOS III programme and grasped the importance of strategic management. In January 2002, the ZOC Board of Directors resolved to undertake a strategic planning process with the help of a Canadian consultant financed by Olympic Solidarity (see next section). The process was led by a steering committee made up of three persons: the secretary general, the chair of the marketing commission, and the operations manager. This committee prepared a ZOC status report and a macro- and micro-environmental scan. A stakeholder survey was circulated to over 60 people. It helped identify ZOC's SWOTs. Input from survey responses was used to plan and design a strategic workshop held in September 2002. This involved 50 ZOC members, staff, and stakeholders. The following strategic framework was adopted at the end of the workshop following sometimes difficult discussions and several drafts.

Mission

To promote and protect the Olympic and Commonwealth Games Movements in Zimbabwe and to facilitate quality participation in the Games.

Vision

The Zimbabwe Olympic Committee facilitates the advancement of high performance sport persons to win Olympic medals in Beijing 2008.

Values

The Zimbabwe Olympic Committee believes in: ethical conduct; transparency and accountability; respect for others; integrity; commitment.

Roles

1. To promote and support Olympism and high performance sport.
2. To ratify and enter the Games Team.
3. To implement Olympic Solidarity Programmes in partnership with National Sports Associations and other stakeholders.
4. To promote fair play, anti-doping and equity in sport.
5. To appoint or nominate representatives to IOC and CGF related positions, fora and programmes.

From this framework a number of priorities and goals were defined, along four lines:

Games

1.1 To ratify the selection, facilitate the final preparation and lead a quality, medal winning team to the Games.

Capacity Building

2.1 To help build the capacity of National Sport Associations in order to increase the number and quality of high performance athletes.

2.2 To be a key partner in the development of an integrated sport system for Zimbabwe.

2.3 To develop and support Zimbabwean sport persons as international leaders in Regional, Continental and International Federation.

2.4 To increase the knowledge, skills experience and number of coaches and sport administrators.

2.5 To provide opportunities for women and athletes in leadership.

Facilitating Athlete Development

3.1 To facilitate the access of high performance athletes to training programmes, International competitions, scholarships and financial resources.

3.2 To educate athletes with respect to Olympism, placing particular emphasis on fair play and anti-doping.

3.3 To facilitate the advancement of female athletes in high performance sport.

3.4 To involve athletes in decision making within ZOC.

Business Development

4.1 To market ZOC to all stakeholders and partners.

4.2 To become an organization that integrates strategic business planning, monitoring and evaluation in all aspects of its business.

4.3 To develop policies, procedures, systems and structures to efficiently manage ZOC.

4.4 To optimize the use of technology.

4.5 To mobilize the financial and human resources necessary to implement the strategic and business plans of ZOC.

After the approval of this framework by the ZOC Board, a business plan and staff work plans were developed, respectively, by the secretary general and the operations manager. These plans are monitored on an ongoing basis by the ZOC Board. Midterm reviews and adjustments will be accomplished by the steering committee and board after the Olympic Games in Athens 2004 and the Commonwealth Games in Melbourne 2006. A final evaluation will be carried out after Beijing 2008.

We are indebted to Joan Duncan of Commonwealth Games Canada for providing the information just presented.

4.7 Olympic Council of Malaysia (OCM)

The OCM, which is the NOC for Malaysia, embarked on it first strategic plan in 1993 (40 years after its inception). The plan covered the period 1993 to 2000 and outlined seven objectives. The implementation of this plan has certainly brought about positive and significant progress and achievements. However, there are clearly unfinished agenda items as well as new challenges, which form the basis of a subsequent strategic plan for 2002 to 2006. For this new period, the decision was made to involve in the strategic planning process as many of the constituents of the OCM as possible. A special committee was appointed to carry out this exercise.

As a first step, a questionnaire was prepared and distributed not only to affiliates but also to other interested parties and stakeholders, including some identified individuals. While the response to the questionnaire was not overwhelming, a number of good ideas and thoughts were indeed picked up that helped in the subsequent planning stages and also served as valuable inputs to the next planned OCM conference. The OCM had initiated the practice of organising an annual thematic conference, and it was decided that for the year 2001 this conference would be dedicated to the strategic planning process. Preparatory work for the conference included preparation of the review of the first strategic plan and its achievements, as well as the guidelines for six workshop groups:

- Image and profile of OCM
- Marketing, sponsorship, and fund-raising
- Organizational structure and management
- Affiliate interest
- Linkage—national and international
- How OCM can improve sport as a discipline

The deliberations of the workshop were recorded by a group of reporters and made available to the Committee for Strategic Planning. The committee worked on these findings through a number of meetings and brainstorming sessions, with the following summary output (See "SWOT Analysis" on p. 33).

The following Vision Statement was subsequently adopted:

As the acknowledged leading agency for sport in the country, the Olympic Council of Malaysia (OCM) will engender and foster Olympic ideals amongst all persons involved in sport and facilitate their participation and assist them in their attainment of excellence at all levels of international competitions in full cooperation with relevant organisations, including the government.

In order to achieve this vision, the strategic plan lists a number of general "strategies" and practical "activities" within these strategies, organised along the six workshop themes. These strategies and activities are regularly reviewed for progress by a Strategic Plan Implementation Committee.

More information relating to this approach can be found at www.olympic.org.my.

We are indebted to Sieh Kok Chi of the Olympic Council of Malaysia for providing the information just presented.

4.8 Olympic Solidarity (OS)

Olympic Solidarity is the department of the IOC that is responsible for the administration and redistribution of funds due the NOCs following the sharing of broadcasting rights for the Olympic Games. This redistribution takes place via several programmes of courses, grants,

SWOT Analysis

Internal analysis	External analysis
Strengths	Opportunities
1. The five rings, which the OCM is associated with remains as one of the world's most marketable symbol. 2. A core of dedicated officials and officers. 3. Assets and savings – building, equities, bonds, etc. 4. International contacts, credibility and goodwill.	1. Capitalise on the current good relations with government agencies. 2. Capitalise on the resurrection of the IOC's image with as new president at the helm. 3. Capitalise on current 'Quiet period' (not having to organise any major competitions) to consolidate OCM.
Weaknesses	Threats
1. Improper organisation that results in peculiarities and inconsistencies leading to a perception of lack of transparency when in reality there is no impropriety. 2. The marketability of the five rings has not been fully exploited here. 3. Shortfall in maximising existing facilities and resources.	1. Crass commercialism threatens to turn both athletes and volunteers into money centered persons whose main drive and expectations will be monetary returns and not all the other altruisms that are the hallmark of Olympism. 2. Culture of entitlement that leads to unbridled expectations.

subsidies, and the like that have evolved over the years since the beginning of the 1980s. These programmes are organised in quadrennial cycles (periods of four years finishing in the year when the Summer Games are organised). Olympic Solidarity is currently at its fifth quadrennial plan, for the years 2001 to 2004. One can consider this the equivalent of the OS strategic plan for this period. This is particularly true since the plan was the occasion for a redefinition of responsibilities between the OS offices in Lausanne and those of the continental associations of NOCs following reflection initiated at the end of Samaranch's presidency (2001) on the part of the Olympic Solidarity Commission, which remains the body with governance over this redistribution system.

After a preface by the new IOC President, the 2001-2004 plan, titled "A Fresh Impetus," recalls the mission and explains the values of OS:

Olympic Solidarity reflects the Olympic ethic of which the basic notions are generosity, understanding and international cooperation, cultural exchanges, the development of sport and its educational aspects and the promotion of a society concerned with human dignity and peace.

The plan then develops the objectives that are common to most of the programmes adopted by OS:

- Promoting the fundamental principles of the Olympic Movement
- Developing the technical sports knowledge of athletes and coaches
- Improving, through scholarships, the technical level of athletes and coaches
- Training sports administrators
- Collaborating with the various IOC Commissions as well as with the organisations and entities pursuing such objectives, particularly through Olympic education and the propagation of sport
- Creating, where needed, simple, functional and economical sports facilities in cooperation with national or international bodies
- Supporting the organisation of competitions at national, regional and continental level under the authority or patronage of the NOCs
- Encouraging joint bilateral or multilateral cooperation programmes among NOCs
- Urging governments and international organisations to include sport in Official Development Assistance.

The 21 worldwide programmes, organised into four areas (athletes, coaches, NOC management, special fields) are then explained in detail, with their respective budgets. The continental programmes are mentioned briefly at the end of the plan.

This strategic plan does not go so far as defining quantitative or qualitative benchmarks.

It nevertheless represents an important step forward in that it makes an overall vision available that should facilitate the management of OS. Annual reports provide the quantitative information for each programme. The quadrennial plan and these reports can be found at www.olympic.org.

Conclusion

In a famous article in the *Harvard Business Review* that appeared in 1987, Mintzberg, one of the best-known authors on management, compared a manager to a potter whose clay is the strategy that he wishes to shape for his organisation. This metaphor permitted Mintzberg to show that formulating and achieving a strategy, like creating a piece of pottery, flow into each other in a fluid process of creative apprenticeship.

Similarly to Mintzberg, could we perhaps, like others (for example, Das [1990]), compare a manager to the coach of a sport team whose game plan constitutes the strategy envisaged? At the same time, we know perfectly well that a game plan developed before the beginning of play must be rapidly adapted to the way the game or match evolves. This is the whole secret of strategic management within teams and Olympic sport organisations and in other forms of collective action: Plan your (strategic) work, but never forget to work your (strategic) plan.

Performance Management of Olympic Sport Organisations

Emmanuel Bayle

University Claude Bernard of Lyon, France, Research Centre for Innovations in Sports

Definition of Performance Management

The central objective of management sciences is research on explanations of factors behind the performance of organisations. Although a great deal of research relating to the management of major companies has been carried out, there is much less available on public and private nonprofit organisations (NPOs) in general and NPOs from the sport movement in particular.

Nevertheless—and whether they are a commercial enterprise, a public entity, or an association—all organisations obtain not only financial, commercial, and image results but also results linked to their statutory objectives and purpose that are not necessarily financial in nature. This is the case for organisations within the Olympic sport movement (clubs, national and international federations, national Olympic committees). These Olympic sport organisations (OSOs) require specific performance management for two main reasons:

- The performance that they seek to attain is not primarily financial. The sport system has social or societal objectives that go beyond these "production" objectives (events, competitions, opportunities to practise sport): participating in the education of citizens, conveying a certain number of values to those actively involved, spreading an ideal message (of peace, educa-

tion, health). This type of project, admittedly with a high ideological dimension, nonetheless theoretically constitutes a dominant and federating purpose for these organisations.

- The decision-taking system is based on volunteerism, that is, unpaid work, and on a democratic governance in which the members theoretically play a fundamental role in terms of participation, management, and control.

In order to understand the expression "performance management," it is necessary to define these two terms:

- The term *management* can be defined as a series of actions for steering, controlling, or activating structures and animating teams. It covers both decision taking and implementing actions. We also speak of the strategic approach that must create the conditions for (economic, technical, social, political) convergence between the organisation and its environment in order for it to achieve its maximum performance potential. Strategic management is based on the organisation's objectives and as a result guides the way in which techniques are implemented in order to serve these objectives.

- The term *performance* was imported some centuries ago from the old French word "performance," that is, to achieve; "performance can be considered the result of action, the action itself or even the success" (Bourguignon, 1995, p. 55). Performance measurement can be carried out by means of a systemic approach (measurement of the performance of external and internal factors behind the results and the results themselves: quality of services, innovation, and flexibility but also sport results) behind the performance of the organisation and its potential performance, or by means of a *managerial* approach (measurement of results obtained in terms of financial results, sport achievements, media coverage, etc).

The expression "managing performance" means *defining, measuring, controlling, and managing the performance of an organisation or of a network of organisations.* This implies proposing tools or operational principles aimed at helping decision makers and managers in their practices regarding strategy, control, performance evaluation (either globally or for a particular service or organisational policy), operations (achieving their tasks), or both of the latter of these.

Figure 5.1 is an attempt to conceptualise the process of managing the performance of an organisation. At the summit, the system of governance theoretically defines, in a formalised or other manner, the strategy of the organisation (vision, mission, objectives), provides the means of achieving this ("operational management," i.e., resource management), and controls the global achievement thereof (performance). It is from this objectively achieved performance and the perception of it by the parties involved ("stakeholders") that the internal and external legitimacy of the organisation and of its system of governance is constructed. The ultimate criteria for performance by any organisation whose actions have a visible impact on society will be the degree of social legitimacy granted to the organisation or its activities by public opinion.

The terms used in figure 5.1 are defined as follows:

- **System of governance:** The actors or entities that take major decisions concerning the organisation (defining strategy, controlling performance, etc.). Generally speaking, the system of governance in nonprofit organisations is legally based on the decisions of its general meeting and their implementation by the executive committee. However, the system may sometimes take the form of a single person, two persons in tandem, or a small group of unpaid or salaried staff (or both) who actually take all strategic decisions.

- **Strategic management:** This denotes the organisation's strategy and mission (theoretically in terms of operational and measurable objectives).

- **Resource management:** This refers to the functions or processes of managing strategy and the implementation of the human, material, and organisational resources necessary to achieve these objectives.

- **System of control:** The system of control refers to strategic control (of whether objectives are achieved), to management (of costs), and to operations (achievement of tasks in the different sectors of work).

- **Performance evaluation:** This denotes the formal control of the organisation's performance (usually annual).

- **Performance achieved ("objectively"):** Performance achieved means the results achieved by the organisation and presented by the organisation at its general assembly.

- **Performance perceived by the stakeholders:** Beyond the objective performance, this refers to the performance as perceived by the stakeholders (members, the relevant ministry with authority, the media) according to their specific objectives. Their perception will influence the degree of balance, stability, and legitimacy of the system and in fact the organisation's capacity to engage with them.

- **Accountability:** This refers to the duty to "account for" the use of funds on the part of the organisation, implying a form of quasi-public transparency and evaluation. This duty is theoretically imperative for associations whose social purpose goes beyond that of providing a service for their members and who, via the achievement of their activities, are seeking to create an impact within society.

- **Legitimacy:** This can be defined by the compatibility of the goals and resources of the organisation with the values of society and can be measured by the degree of social legitimacy

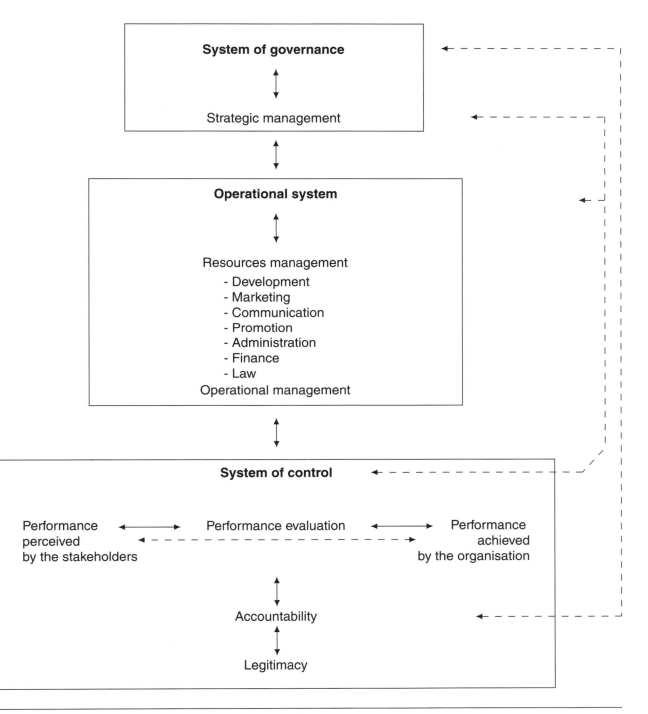

→ Essential relations between management concepts

◂ – → Retroaction (reciprocal influence of performance factors or concepts).

System of governance

Strategic management

Operational system

Resources management
- Development
- Marketing
- Communication
- Promotion
- Administration
- Finance
- Law
Operational management

System of control

Performance perceived by the stakeholders

Performance evaluation

Performance achieved by the organisation

Accountability

Legitimacy

Figure 5.1 The performance management system within an organisation.

granted to the organisation or to its activities by public opinion.

The purpose of the next chapters is to present the application of performance management concepts to Olympic sport organisations (OSOs) and the implications that such an application can have for those managing these organisations.

A process involving several stages is proposed in order to provide an understanding of performance management in OSOs:

- Defining the concept of *"performance"* for Olympic sport organisations (notably by trying to define their legitimate needs or the expectations they must meet)

- Identifying the *system for evaluating and controlling this performance*

- Determining the *conditions for steering this performance:* the strategic principles, the coordination of organisational networks, the rules concerning decision making and concrete actions within the various areas of activity, and the coordination between the work of unpaid and salaried staff.

six

Measuring the Performance of Olympic Sport Organisations

In this chapter we begin by presenting the context and stakes for measuring the performance of Olympic sport organisations (OSOs). Secondly we define the concept of performance for sport organisations. Then we consider "theoretical" measurement models and "empirical" measurement means. Given the limitations of these two types of measurement, we present two examples of measuring performance; both use an approach based on taking into account the expectations of the various sport stakeholders. The first example is of measurement aimed at establishing a typology of performance by several national sport federations (NSFs) at a given moment, and the second is an example of measuring the performance of a sport federation over time.

6.1 The Context and Stakes for OSOs

Sport activity has traditionally been organised around the commitment of volunteers alone who combined the qualities of a leader in the political sense of the term, of an administrator in the sense of a manager, of a moderator, and of a sport technician. Despite this historical fact, all analysis of the sport world has stressed the unavoidable evolution of OSOs *toward concerns linked to managerial issues.* These concerns evolved from far-reaching changes in the *environment.* The changes have included new opportunities *but also threats and uncertainties* that appeared after the 1980s: the increased power of statutory constraints (in most countries); the arrival of private financial investors imposing greater demands; the evolution of the role of public authorities (less financial and more statutory); competition to sport clubs and federations by commercial enterprises, notably regarding services supplied; and the organisation of sport events. Finally, a new and more individualist sport culture has, for some 30 years now, been questioning the legitimacy of the structures that are representative of the sport movement.

Today, the sport organisation must manage relations with partners (the State, local and regional authorities, commercial enterprises, broadcasters, etc.) with multiple and diverging—or even contradictory—interests. Its objectives and methods of intervention may undergo changes as a consequence and can thus appear to be badly defined or lacking in coherence. Moreover, evaluation of the pertinence of resources deployed is often difficult to perform without a clear vision of how these organisations are steered and without a management tool that is specifically adapted to suit sport organisations.

In this context, the question of evaluating the efficiency and performance of OSOs and notably their representative structures, the NSFs or international federations (IFs) and national Olympic committees (NOCs) or unions of continental federations, becomes more and more legitimate. Whether via discovering cases of misappropriated funds, highly precarious financial situations, internal political conflicts that are given major media coverage, or management practices that are contested because of their lack of transparency, the conditions for managing these bodies and their effectiveness began to be seriously questioned during the 1990s. Even the International Olympic Committee came under considerable attention and pressure in 1999 due to doping and corruption affairs, and had to adapt its rules and membership (see Chappelet 2001).

For this reason, an effort (as required by other private and public organisations) to provide transparency and effectiveness in their management practices is often demanded of OSOs by their "partners," those who provide resources, and by their principal agents, that is, the clubs and licensed athletes in the sports concerned.

The performances by athletes from certain nations at the Olympic Games or major international competitions, as well as the spectacular progress in the number of licensed athletes and in the budget of some national and international federations, raise questions in the mind of a manager trying to understand how organisations in the sport sector are structured and led; where the resources come from; what management principles are used; and how one can explain the results obtained.

The notion of performance for an organisation appears to be composite. It can be reflected in several ways—that is, in economic terms (growth of the organisation), financial terms (profitability), and organisational or even social terms. It is also clear that any appreciation of the performance of any organisation demands a multicriteria approach. However, the OSOs combine mixed and paradoxical types of logic of intervention and functioning: original associative logic, often "public service" logic (in most countries where a ministry of sport exists), and commercial logic.

Commercial logic in the world of OSOs can be explained by several factors:

- *The emergence of a professional sphere* and an intensification of the financial issues at stake within elite sport, competitions, and sport in general could lead in the long term to a risk of eviction of the federations, and on a larger scale sport organisations, from their market of the most lucrative competitions (see Bayle and Durand 2000).

- A change in modes of consumption regarding sport practices. *In developed countries, this takes* the form of a stagnation in the practice of traditional sports as a licensed athlete, a growing demand for availability of sports, multiple forms of competition within sport, a growing number of sports and types of practice, and the appearance of alternative forms of practice that form the basis of a new sporting culture (see Loret 1995; Chifflet 1987, 1995; Ramanantsoa and Thiery-Baslé 1989; Guay 1997).

One of the major issues at stake for the sport movement is taking into account and responding to new demands regarding sport practice. The problem is the very difficulty of clearly identifying the new expectations that escape any attempt at planning and contractualisation because of their unpredictable, transient character. New practices are oriented toward several aspects at once: a process of mass involvement and of diversification and increasing segmentation due to the effect of (and individualisation of) the demand for sport that is undergoing a move toward natural, open terrain and more generally toward open-air, leisure sport (mountain biking, climbing, hiking, etc.).

- *An evolution of the role of public authority.* Ministries or State departments have increasingly fewer resources for reducing inequalities among the NSFs. Although they admittedly represent essential sources of financing for some, they position themselves—depending on political pressures—more and more as a partner and regulator of the environment of the NSFs and of their statutory and regulatory functioning.

Faced with a context that is becoming ever more competitive because of pressure brought to bear by the various commercial actors (organisers of events, sport practicers, manufacturers of sport items and equipment, television), an increasingly heterogeneous and uncertain internal situation is developing within the system of each individual sport federation and within the sport movement as a whole:

- The situation for *each individual sport federation's system* is changing because of cultural factors within the management of relations between tradition and modernity, the new versus the traditional sporting culture, nonprofit as opposed to profitability, and so on. This heterogeneous situation generates differing visions on the part of the actors involved regarding conditions for the development of sport and the goals that the organisations should strive for.

- The situation within *the sport movement as a whole* explains the different potential for economic development for each discipline—some sports are "winners" while others are "losers."

The issue is thus to establish a range of practices and, more globally, of services adapted to a demand that includes varying needs, and to present a clearer strategy to the various potential financial partners (television, private and public partners). More precisely, the question that has been facing the OSOs for about 10 years is whether they are, and will be, capable of managing and integrating these centrifugal

kinds of logic (notably commercial, etc.) while maintaining a certain degree of coherence (notably cultural) within a federation's system. If the tendencies of the sector to evolve incite the OSOs' administrators and executives to integrate a commercial approach, a federation's global strategy must in fact combine several kinds of logic for development when defining—and above all when implementing—the essential interplay of ambiguity, paradoxes, and compromises.

The evolution of the national federations and NOCs reveals that their positioning now takes place on a triple scale that requires these organisations to find a balance between three functioning kinds of logic (associative, public, and commercial) that are contradictory yet paradoxically complementary for development, which must include managing compromises. This is illustrated in figure 6.1.

For organisations whose purpose is not primarily to make a profit, the absence of a synthetic measurement of global performance such as the profits achieved, as well as the difficulty of measuring social and humanistic objectives (development of the human being, promotion of humanistic values via the practice of sport, etc.), makes the measurement and the steering of performance more complex.

The origins of performance can be multiple and complex to determine for organisations whose interactions with the environment are

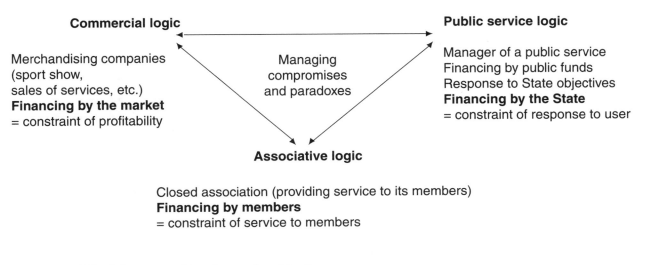

Figure 6.1 Managing compromises between three principles of functioning.

so considerable and multiple. Moreover, for this type of organisation with a political functioning, is it possible to legitimise the strategies and the modes of organisation by the desire to seek performance? The response might not necessarily be affirmative.

6.2 The Concept of Performance for OSOs

Traditionally, performance measurement is understood to be an a posteriori evaluation of the results obtained by an organisation, but much research work has also presented it as the measurement of factors behind performance. This explains the confusion between measuring results and measuring the factors behind the origins of these results.

According to Lorino (1999, p. 27), it is possible to say that "in the notion of performance, we always find the value/cost ratio, designated according to context by the ratios of quality/price, utility/price, differentiation/leadership-cost, efficiency/effectiveness." Although there is great confusion within the literature on management between the terms "performance" and "effectiveness," the term "performance" is today used much more frequently by scholars. Effectiveness is traditionally defined as the degree to which organisational objectives are achieved or as the capacity to create acceptable results and actions. For this reason, effectiveness always appears relative to projects by one or several actors, whether within or related to an organisation. Efficiency, on the other hand, has to do with comparison of the resources used and effective production, independently of any satisfaction felt by the user.

In the case of a for-profit company, financial value no doubt constitutes the ultimate goal or at least the synthetic measurement of performance and the main objective to be achieved. Revealing a composite performance for a nonprofit organisation (NPO) in which the notion of efficiency is not predominant, and in which effectiveness is a complex construction with a strong external connotation ("societal performance"), imposes reflection on the appropriate type of performance measurement to adopt. We define societal performance as the social and economic contribution of the OSO's

system toward the smooth running of society (see Bayle 1999; Massiera 1998; Fatoux and Tiberghien 2004).

As long as an OSO manages to procure the financial and human resources that are necessary for it to function, ensuring a maximum degree of efficiency can in the end be of relatively low importance. For an association, inefficiency or even a lack of effectiveness is not necessarily problematic as long as the members do not express dissatisfaction regarding the inertia and if the association manages to preserve a relative financial equilibrium. The lack of performance, in fact, represents a lesser danger than it would for a company. The disciplinary mechanisms are less present. The survival of the organisation is rarely at stake.

Moreover, the social or societal objectives that are priorities in these organisations can explain the lack of a preponderance of efficiency indicators. For this reason, it is clear that the performance of an NPO is expected to be more one of effectiveness than of efficiency. However, for private NPOs, controlling their results is much more complex given that the objectives are qualitative and often impossible to reflect in concrete terms. In addition, the absence of a dominant objective makes it difficult to evaluate private NPOs based on a synthetic indicator. It is sometimes possible to discover organisations whose objective is a commercial one under the cover of private NPOs, and whose ultimate purpose is to increase their financial basis; the constraint of nondistribution of profit can, in practice, be circumvented.

The performance of a private NPO can be understood as its capacity to acquire and use human, material, and financial resources in order to achieve its (statutory and ideological) objectives. Performance in this case also corresponds to the judgment issued by its many stakeholders—individuals or groups, depending on their representation—of the services, results, and effects they expect of the organisation (which implies a subjective measurement of performance). For this reason, measuring the performance of a private NPO must combine objective and subjective measurements in order to provide a richer and more real vision of the global performance. However, one of the great difficulties involved consists of measuring the external effects on the NPO's activities. These questions on the definition of the performance of private NPOs in general and sport organisations in particular raise the question of the type of measurement to adopt. We shall study the theoretical methods that are possible and the empirical methods currently practised within OSOs.

6.3 Theoretical and Empirical Measurement Models

Evaluating the performance of a federation of associations (as many OSOs are) raises a specific problem that is more complex than simply the evaluation of the performance of an association, because it is a question of also measuring the performance of a network of organisations (the sport system, IFs, national federations, regional leagues, area committees, and clubs, plus commercial structures to which certain organisations within the sport movement belong as members or of which they are the single stakeholders).

The performance of the organisation is recognised by scholars and practitioners as a multidimensional concept, whether this concerns an association, a company, or a public organisation; but we see this question as most problematic for a private NPO. We shall show (a) that even with a multidimensional approach, the evaluation methods are not necessarily suitable for measuring the performance of sport organisations, and (b) that ("empirical") methods currently used for measuring performance are also not necessarily satisfactory.

Theoretical Methods

We have attempted to classify methods of measuring performance based on four classical means of measurement (the degree of achieving objectives, the resources system, internal functioning, strategic components) and four more holistic approaches: competitive values (Quinn and Rohrbaugh 1981, 1983; the four-dimensional model (Morin et al. 1994); the six-dimensional model for service organisations (Fitzgerald et al. 1994); and the balanced scorecard (Kaplan and Norton 1996). These methods are presented in table 6.1, as is their operationality for the OSOs.

Table 6.1 **Methods of Measuring the Global Performance of an Organisation and Its Applicability for Measuring the Performance of Olympic Sport Organisations**

Measurement model (main authors)	Concept of performance	Interest of using this model (conditions of validity)	Limitations to use with regard to the specificity of OSOs	Opera-tionality for OSOs[1]
Degree of achiev-ing objectives (Steers 1975; Hall 1980)	Achieving fixed objectives	The goals are clear, are limited in time, and can be measured.	The goals are unclear, sometimes somewhat unrealistic and variable according to the life cycle of the organisation. -	—
Resource system (Penrose 1959; Wernerfelt 1984)	Acquiring the funda-mental resources for organisational func-tioning	A clear connection exists between the input and output data.	Certain resources come from the supervisory authority and are renewed annually. —	-
Internal function-ing (Argyris 1964; Das 1990)	Absence of internal tension, regular inter-nal functioning with regard to objective(s) to be achieved	A clear connection exists between the organisational functioning and the organi-sational objectives.	This is not the same connection as that for a company. —	-

(continued)

Table 6.1 *(continued)*

Measurement model (main authors)	Concept of performance	Interest of using this model (conditions of validity)	Limitations to use with regard to the specificity of OSOs	Opera-tionality for OSOs[1]
Strategic components (Connoly, Conlon, and Deutsch 1980)	At least minimal satisfaction with the principal strategic components	The component groups have considerable influence on the organisation, which must respond to their expectations. The main strategic groups are those whom it is most legitimate to satisfy.	Highly pertinent in proportion to the authority of the Ministry of Youth and Sport Difficult to implement in order to determine the views of all components (in terms of feasibility and time) Problem of retaining only subjective data +	+
Competitive values (Quinn and Rohrbaugh 1981, 1983)	Evaluation of the organisation in four principal domains must meet those favoured by the components	The organisation experiences uncertainties regarding its own evaluations; the evaluation criteria evolve according to the phase in the organisation's life cycle.	Difficult to implement and not really applicable to nonprofit organizations. —	—
Four-dimensional model (Morin 1989, 1994)	Systemic evaluation of performance	The organisation's performance is measured by a subjective and objective approach. Measurement of legitimacy.	Measurement of legitimacy +	-
Six-dimensional model for service organisations (Fitzgerald et al. 1994)	Systemic evaluation of performance	Two areas (results and determinants) and six dimensions (two dimensions for results: competitiveness and financial performance; for determinant factors: quality of service, flexibility, resource utilisation, innovation)	Possibility of adapting for nonprofit organizations ++	++
Balanced score-card (Kaplan 1999; Kaplan and Norton 2001)	Systemic evaluation of performance	Four main strategic dimensions to set up an organizational balance scorecard (finances, customer relations, internal processes, learning and growth)	Possibility of adapting for nonprofit organizations ++	++

[1]We denote the interest of using the method as follows: — = no interest; - = limited interest; + = of interest, ++ = ideas or methodology to be adopted.

As table 6.1 illustrates, the typology of the theoretical approaches to measuring the performance of OSOs that we have established must not exclude the fact that many researchers on the measurement of performance by OSOs retain or link several perspectives, or can be situated at the border of different approaches that were adopted to measure the global performance of an organisation. Most of the relevant approaches to the measurement of organisa- tional performance in the sport management literature (Frisby 1986; Vail 1986; Chelladurai et al. 1987; Paradimitriou 1994; Koski 1995; Madella 1998; Bayle 2000; Esposito and Madella 2003) are based on a simple and normalized procedure consisting of identification of a set of dimensions of performance and, within these, of a range of criteria or performance indicators for all the different dimensions. Identification of dimensions has been carried out on the basis of very different theoretical assumptions, ranging from the system resource model to the strategic constituency approach, the goal achievement model, or more balanced or holistic approaches like the competing values model or stakeholder-based models. Table 6.2 summarises these approaches.

Table 6.2 **Results of Methods for Measuring the Performance of Olympic Sport Organisations**

Authors	Method of measurement	Sample	Results	Interests	Limitations
Chelladurai et al. (1987)	Internal functioning (empirical and quantitative study of the concept of performance for NSFs)	Questionnaire of 30 indicators applied to 150 executives from 48 Canadian national federations	• Proposal for a model with six dimensions • Dimensions for results of elite and masses not at all linked • Most critical dimensions: transformation process, the human resources factor, and the results of the elite programmes	Pertinence of the methodology	• Measurement of the quality of functioning more than of the results • Specificity of the Canadian context (very strong financial dependence of NSFs) • Measurement of internal data and results over the same period
Frisby (1986)	System of resources and system of achieving objectives	Quantitative study (sample unknown)	Study of the relation between structure and effectiveness	Definition of indicators for the NSFs	Variables of performance measurement of NSFs not taken into account
Koski (1995)	System of resources (study of environmental/ functional link and effectiveness of sport club)	Quantitative study (835/6,500 questionnaires sent to club directors)	• Definition of five factors for effectiveness of a club • Dimensions correlated • Highlighting the variation of effectiveness in a cyclical manner	Systemic approach to variables influencing performance	• Synchronic measurement of variables • Measurements on the club (purpose different from that of an NSF)
Vail (1986)	Strategic components (multidimensional study of the concept of performance)	Five strategic groups used (140 questionnaires, 33 NSFs)	Six dimensions (36 criteria) of performance: adaptability, communication, finances, growth, human resources, and organisational planning	Significant difference in the importance of the criteria for the effectiveness of the organisation between internal and external groups for the growth and finance variables (internal groups perceive these variables as more crucial)	• Essential indicators not taken into account in measuring performance: sport results, number of members, etc.

(continued)

Table 6.2　*(continued)*

Authors	Method of measurement	Sample	Results	Interests	Limitations
Papad-imitriou (1994)	Strategic components	Six strategic component groups, applied to 20 Greek NSFs	• Five dimensions of effectiveness revealed: balance of executive committee and external relations, attention paid to athletes, internal procedures, long-term planning, and contribution of science toward sport; 33 measurement indicators • Athletes and support staff the least satisfied with the effectiveness of the NSFs, and members of the executive committee the most satisfied	Measurement of the organisation's legitimacy toward its main components (satisfaction of the actors)	• Problem with the reliability and validity of this method • Operational-ity problematic because process long and incurs high costs
Papad-imitriou and Taylor (2000)	Strategic components	Five strategic component groups (423 respondents) to measure board effec-tiveness (indicator of organizational performance of Greek NSFs)	• Technical staff, elite ath-letes less satisfied than board members and international officials with quality of Greek NSOs' governance • Administrative paid staff appeared more satis-fied with leadership of NSOs • Small NSOs' boards better in satisfying their constituent groups	Measure-ment of the organisation's governance legitimacy toward its main components	Just focused on board functioning
Madella (1998)	Multidi-mensional approach (degree of achieving objectives, the resource system, inter-nal functioning, strategic com-ponents)	Mix of quanti-tative informa-tion (statistical data, etc.) and percep-tion of stake-holders	Performance measurement of a single federation (Italian athletics, 11 performance dimensions (114 indicators): finances; human resources; inter-organisational rela-tions; athletes' performance (international level); ath-letes' performance (national level); quality of services; production of events; inter-nal communication; technol-ogy, logistics, and produc-tion factors; production of knowledge; and flexibility and innovation	Mix of practical and theoretical interest (score-board)	Difficulty of adapting system to political changes and priori-ties

(continued)

Table 6.2 *(continued)*

Authors	Method of measurement	Sample	Results	Interests	Limitations
Esposito and Madella (2003)	Multidimensional approach (systemic evaluation)	Mix of quantitative information (statistical data, etc.) and perceptions of stakeholders and strategic themes and priorities of the federation over four years (1997-2001 and 2001-2004)	Performance measurement of a single federation (Italian athletics) over time; seven performance dimensions (111 indicators Results obtained in international and national competitions, (voluntary) human resources/clients (members, coaches, etc.), marketing and communication, volume and quality of services delivered to users directly by the federation or indirectly by the affiliated clubs, economic and financial performance, internal process (including communication and technology), innovation and organizational learning	Mix of practical and theoretical interest (score-board) Evolution of Madella's model	
Bayle (1999, 2000)	Multidimensional approach (managerial evaluation)	Mix of quantitative information (statistical data, etc.) and perceptions of stakeholders	Measurement of the performance of 40 French national federations in 1992/1993 and 1996/1997 Six performance dimensions: statutory, internal social, societal, economic and financial, promotional, organisational (65 indicators)	Mix of practical and theoretical interest	No systemic evaluation (input variables)

Empirical Measurements

One can identify seven empirical methods of performance evaluation for an OSO like an NSF. The characteristics of these methods are presented in table 6.3.

For national sport federations, three methods have a mandatory character. These are political (or statutory); legal from an accounting and financial point of view; and sometimes legal and conventional (carried out by the supervisory authority, generally, the Ministry of Sport). The other four methods are not mandatory and are consequently much more informal, but may have an impact on the statutory methods. It should also be noted that these evaluation methods have a clear form of interaction, which can generate new priorities and thus attention to new performance criteria for each evaluating body depending on the relative importance of each.

However, none of these principles and methods present genuine guarantees of a global, exhaustive, and impartial understanding of the performance of a federation. Moreover, evaluation of an NSF's performance cannot be objective because two conditions are missing:

• The possibility of comparing results with competing bodies

• Calling on independent experts, a notion raised by scholars (Le Duff and Papillon 1997) as the prerequisite for a genuine, complete, and critical evaluation of the performance of a public or private NPO

Finally, it appears globally that the main method of evaluating OSOs like national

Table 6.3 **Empirical Methods of Evaluating the Performance of a National Sport Federation**

Methods of evaluation	Political (or statutory)	Legal and conventional	Legal (accounting and financial viewpoint)	Supra-national system of adhesion	Conventional and contractual	Media attraction	Managerial
Evaluation criteria	Qualitative and quantitative	Mainly quantitative	Quantitative	Rather quantitative	Qualitative and quantitative	Qualitative and quantitative	Quantitative, qualitative
Evaluating organism	General assembly (members of the federation)	Ministry of Sport	Certified accountant/auditor	International federation (+ IOC)	(1) External partner, sponsors, multisport federations, etc. (2) Salaried employees of federation	Media: specialised sport papers (and to a lesser degree national television channels)	The managerial system (volunteer and/or salaried staff in charge of the association)
Level of evaluation	Federation's internal system	Supervisory authority	Independent body	International authority	(1) "External co-contractants" (2) "Internal co-contractants"	External bodies, public opinion	Internal
Type of evaluation	Formalised	Formalised	Formalised	Not formalised	Formalised	Not formalised	Formalised or not formalised
Period of evaluation	Annual (in principle every four years at the elective level)	Annual	Annual	Variable	Variable (according to the terms of the contract) and depending on the evolution of the interests of the contractants	Variable (stronger in periods of crisis or just before significant sport events such as the Olympic Games or World Championships)	Variable according to sectors evaluated (according to the technocratic culture)

federations is of a political nature, whether at the statutory level (the members) or the conventional level on the part of its supervisory body (ministry of sport, IF) or the media.

Following a synthesis of previous research and empirical measurement methods, *we did not find methods without shortcomings on the level of validity, reliability, and operationality.* We are obliged to accept the pertinence of the strategic components approach because of the attention it pays to the parties involved, and of the approach developed by Morin et al. (1994) for its general perspective and for a certain number of indicators proposed by previous researchers regarding the performance of OSOs. The choice of indicators is in fact the responsibility of the director of the organisation or of individuals who are experts in the sector.

The "how to evaluate," however, depends to a large extent on the question of "why evaluate." Among all these approaches dedicated to measuring the concept of organisational performance, there is the risk of confusing the performance that is an effect or a result (or both) with what determines the mechanisms of a result.

6.4 Presentation of Measurement Methods for OSOs

It is possible to try to evaluate the performance of an organisation over time or of several organisations at a given moment.

We present two different areas of work on measurement: one based on a managerial approach to performance and the other based on a systemic approach to measuring performance. The first is a typological approach that aimed to compare the performance of several federations at the beginning and the end of the 1990s (Bayle 1999). The second corresponds to performance measurement of an athletics federation over time (Madella 1998; Esposito and Madella 2003).

Both these methods are based on a stakeholder approach to defining performance indicators, which we describe first.

A Stakeholder Approach to Defining Performance Indicators

In order to grasp the indicators of an NSF's global performance, it is first necessary to analyse the expectations of the various stakeholders. We feel that this stage is necessary in order to build up all the criteria for an "objective" performance measurement. It may also reveal the imbalance between some specific expectations and the results actually obtained, thus allowing a better understanding of the organisation's dysfunctions.

In accordance with the approach taken by Spriggs (1994), we have chosen to take into account, within our performance evaluation process, the expectations of the stakeholders and of the direct public. In figure 6.2 we show the many different expectations of the NSF on the part of the various stakeholders. These expectations make it possible to identify the implicit or explicit criteria for performance that give rise to the mechanisms for evaluating performance.

All the stakeholders listed have variable interests depending on the life cycle of the organisation (growth, decline, etc.). We base our statement on the hypothesis that the more the federation is dependent on a specific source of financing (members, Ministry of Sport, or one or more sponsors), the more important it becomes to satisfy the expectations of this main financial source. Moreover, the network strategy becomes inevitably more and more complex as the association grows.

Based on interviews and documentary analysis of NSFs, we defined the expectations and measurement indicators for each stakeholder. Table 6.4 shows, as an example, what could be the expectations of a Ministry of Sport—an essential stakeholder of many NSFs.

The expectations of each stakeholder, listed in this way, give rise to specific performance evaluation models (see section 6.3, "Theoretical and Empirical Measurement Models").

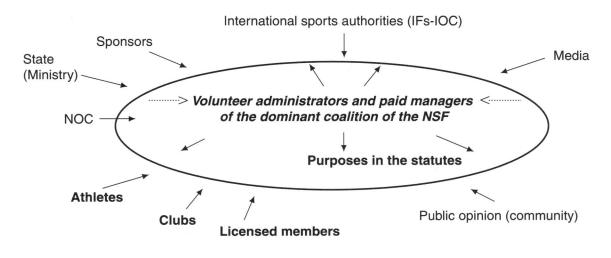

Figure 6.2 Main actors with expectations of a national sport federation.

Table 6.4 **Expectations of the Ministry of Sport From a National Sport Federation**

What the Ministry of Sport expects from an NSF	Possible indicators
Economic and financial	
• Financial equilibrium of NSFs receiving grants • (Relative) autonomy of financing • Respect for fiscal, social, and accounting rules • Financial transparency • Respect for statutory obligations	• Accounting results (net situation/assets on balance sheet) • Ratio of dependence on Ministry of Youth and Sport • Number of "disputes" or incidents justifying the intervention of the ministry in the NSF • Financial and accounting procedures • Situation regarding fiscal and/or social recovery • Truthfulness of the financial elements communicated, acceptance of control procedures
Societal	
• Creation of jobs linked to the sport discipline • Economic development linked to the sports in question • Socialisation via sport and reduction of juvenile delinquency	• Number of jobs created (coaches, etc.) in the sport discipline • Progression of turnover by national sport industries • Direct and indirect economic impact linked to the discipline concerned • Number of young people in difficult areas of towns or in difficulty who are reintegrated via sport
Sport politics	
• Development (institutional) of sport practice and quality opportunities throughout national territory • Development of support and coaching for those practising the sport • More generally, and unspoken, enhancing the image of the political party in power • National representation in the major "significant" competitions	• Growth in the number of licensed athletes, clubs on a national, regional, and area level • Number of volunteers, number of those holding State certification (active in their profession) • Quality of element of attraction to media that promotes the political party in power • Number of medals won (mainly at the Olympic Games, World Championships, etc.) for the senior teams

Typology for Measuring the Performance of the NSFs

The objective of the study presented here was to establish a typology of the performance profiles of NSFs based on a global measurement of the performance of each NSF (see Bayle 1999). The aim was to explain the differences in performance among federations (see Tomé 2002). We therefore needed a grid to permit comparisons between them.

Performance Dimensions and Indicators

Based on the expectations of the stakeholders, the performance indicators were grouped around six dimensions, validated by a panel of experts: statutory performance (sports), organi-

sational performance, financial performance, promotional performance, internal social performance, and societal performance.

Evaluating the performance via the six dimensions made it possible to create a global measurement of a federation's performance based on a multidimensional image of the federation as illustrated in table 6.5. This table defines the six dimensions and the possible means of measuring them.

In order to understand the global performance of an organisation, some authors identify types of performance that can be qualified as intermediary or internal (organisational performance, social performance, etc.); these concern the way in which the organisation is structured (interfunctional integration, seeking flexibility, etc.) in order to achieve the final performance expected. These intermediary performances can

Table 6.5 **Measuring the Global Performance of National Sport Federations**

Dimensions	Statutory (sports)	Internal social	Societal	Economic and financial	Promotional	Organisational
Objectives	Obtaining the best sport results (national teams), developing the number of members	Improving the social climate and the involvement of all actors concerned	Contributing, by achieving their statutory objective, toward a better-functioning society	• Obtaining the resources necessary to achieve the statutory objective • Managing their financial dependence (notably regarding the supervisory authority)	Improving the media impact of the discipline among those practising this sport and the public	Organising, internally at headquarters and within the system, to respond to their statutory mission, to the strategic plan, and to the requirements of the environment
Means	Measurement of the sport results at high level and the number of licensed athletes	Measurement of the degree of satisfaction of the actors	Measurement of the societal legitimacy and the impact of the federation's activities on society	Measurement of the capacity to obtain financial resources, diversification of resources, the capacity for self-financing	Measurement of the reputation and the image	Measurement of the quality of functioning and the organisational reactivity
Method of measurement	Quantitative and qualitative	Qualitative	Qualitative	Quantitative	Quantitative and qualitative	Qualitative

also make it possible to understand the organisation's potential performance. We also need to note that the dimensions identified do not intervene at the same stage of the organisation's functioning. The organisational and social indicators are rather more internal, while the statutory, economic, financial, external social, and promotional indicators are more reflective of the exchanges between the organisation and its environment.

Achieving a statutory purpose is more complex for a federation of associations than for a single association. For a federation, it calls upon all the members (clubs) of the federation and its decentralised bodies (leagues and area committees). For this reason, the statutory performance of federations resides in the large number of small associations that are seeking to achieve their objectives.

The major difficulty in measuring economic and financial performance is isolating the economic and financial performance of the federation's system from that of the federation in the strict sense of the word. If the financial performance of a sport federation is relatively easy to determine by studying its accounts, that of the sport discipline is much more complex because of the complexity of understanding all the resources generated. A comparison among the federations thus becomes difficult to achieve without use of the same measurement units. For example, the French tennis federation manages directly, and on behalf of the federation, the French Open Tennis Tournament (Roland Garros), while professional football is managed by a professional league (Ligue Nationale de Football), which is autonomous.

It is therefore necessary to exercise prudence in conducting comparative analysis of federations' financial performances, given the strategic, legal, and accounting choices that are at times different.

The external social or societal performance corresponds to the contribution, notably in the social (or economic) sense, of the NSF to society (contribution to citizens' health, education, and more globally their well-being, contribution to economic development, etc.). The difficulty here consists of measuring the "real" social and economic impact of the activities implemented by an NSF. This requires a response to the following questions: What does an Olympic medal or a title at World Championships mean for the country? What are the benefits to the community of practising sports in terms of improving public health or preventing ill health? What are, in reality, the specific values conveyed by sport among those practising it for themselves (or for those close to them), and what is the benefit that society derives regarding social cohesion, well-being, and the like?[1]

Here, the complexity stems from the fact that societal performance corresponds to the contribution of the federation's system toward the smooth running of society, which in turn leads to a legitimacy performance measured by the degree of legitimacy attributed to the organisation and to its actions by society. The requirements of the environment, and notably of the State, may moreover incite the NSF, like all organisations, to be responsible for the societal issues to an extent that goes beyond its statutory objective.

For each of the dimensions, Bayle (1999) constructed items to explain the performance dimensions identified from interviews, from the questionnaire used in the preliminary investigation, from previous research, and from the expectations of the various stakeholders. A test of the questionnaire with a panel of experts was then carried out. The questionnaire was modified accordingly and then sent (in 1993 and then a second time in 1998) to 53 directors of single-sport federations with over 5,000 licensed members whose disciplines were recognised by the Ministry of Youth and Sport as high-level disciplines.

The final sample consisted of 40 federations, of which 22 were Olympic federations and 18 were non-Olympic; the response rate was 75.5%. All the larger federations were represented in our investigation.

The person replying to the questionnaire was asked to evaluate the performance in 1997 but also over the period 1992/1993, since we wished to identify an approach to performance measurement at two different moments. The period between 1992/1993 and 1997 corresponds to a cycle that is longer than an Olympiad, that is, a period during which changes are likely to appear (evolution of sport results, changes to management, arrival or departure of a major financial partner, etc.). We knew that such a perspective of evaluation would be difficult and would have limitations to the extent that calling upon memory and the risk of self-justifying judgments are delicate areas of bias when one is implementing qualitative methods.

The performance measurement questionnaire sent to directors utilised a seven-degree scale, as generally recommended by specialists (Cox 1980). This odd-numbered scale with a numerical anchor from 1 to 7 makes it possible to provide a neutral response.

A questionnaire specifically developed for an expert on the activities of the federations, who was in charge of the single-sport federations within the Ministry of Youth and Sport, was drawn up to measure societal performance. The evaluation by this expert covers both 1997 and the period 1992/1993.

Two questionnaires were developed for two other experts on the federations' systems: the director of Olympic preparation and the person in charge of elite sports at the Ministry of Sport. These respondents were to interpret the objective data (sport results for French teams in international competitions and evolution of licensed athletes) in order to develop an appreciation of specific performance by the federations. We chose to retain, as a measurement period, the period between 1988 and 1997 because the experts consulted had data available to carry out this evaluation.

The subjective data thus come from a total of four questionnaires. All the "subjective" indicators made it possible to measure the relative performance of the federation depending on the official objectives of the federation, in a given context, and at its stage of evolution.

---

[1]For example, after the victory of the French football team in the 1998 World Cup, the media spoke of a "World Cup effect" that was positive for the morale and confidence of the population (the spectacular progression of the confidence scale of householders as surveyed by the National Survey Institute INSEE in July 1998, the highest level achieved since 1986, was attributed in part to this victory. Even if this indicator can be questioned, the social and economic impact of the French team victory seems to have had a psychological effect on the French population.

As a complement to the qualitative measurements, "objective" indicators were also retained. These "objective" indicators make it possible to measure the gross or absolute performance, which we reprocessed on a scale from 1 to 7 based on a specific rule of calculation.

For the objective data, we generally adopted a 10-year measurement period (1988-1997) in order to achieve a better analysis of how the federation's performance evolved. This choice can be justified by the fact that certain indicators are useful only if they are evaluated over a long period (this is the case for the evolution in the number of licensed athletes or the sport results, or even the evolution of results obtained).

For example, when measuring performance in terms of licensed athletes, seven items were retained: five subjective (three evaluated by the director, two by an expert) and two objective. One item, performance in terms of licensed athletes and their evolution, was evaluated by three methods of measurement. For elite athletes, three subjective items were retained: one evaluated by the director for Olympic preparation and two by the director of elite sport at the Ministry of Youth and Sport. See table 6.6.

To measure economic and financial performance, seven objective indicators and seven subjective indicators were used (see table 6.7).

To measure the social and economic contribution of the federation's system to society, it would be possible to retain the methods used by economists, notably the cost–benefit method or economic impact studies. Evaluation of the socioeconomic benefits for practising athletes or those close to them can be carried out using a "cost–benefit" method (the benefit being the sum of satisfaction obtained by beneficiaries from a programme). One can also measure the societal performance of the NSFs' activities using the "social effects" method (whereby one studies the extent to which the federations' services meet social demands). Here, the aim is to pinpoint the effects on the beneficiaries, beyond their satisfaction alone and taking into account the modifications that have arisen through their "consumption of the service." The effect of this is considered at the level of the beneficiary but also those close to them. For this reason, it appears very difficult to evaluate the social effects. Measuring the impact of the NSFs' activities (notably the economic effects) could also be carried out via "impact studies."

Quantitative studies of this type—whether to measure the socioeconomic impact of the federation's activities on the civil population or on the licensed athletes—do not exist. At our level, and for evident reasons, we were not able to undertake such projects. Faced with methodological difficulties, we evaluated social

Table 6.6 **Examples of Statutory Performance Indicators**

Variable to be measured	Indicator retained	Source of information
Capacity to attract and keep licensed athletes (and evolution of numbers)	• Number of members (size in number of licensed athletes) • Evolution of number of licensed athletes between 1988 and 1997 • Evaluation of the number of licensed athletes by an expert from the Ministry of Youth and Sport in 1997 • Evaluation by an expert from the Ministry of Youth and Sport on the evolution of the number of licensed athletes between 1988 and 1997	Statistics from the Ministry of Youth and Sport (reprocessed on a scale of 1-7)
Capacity to obtain sport results by senior elite teams at the Olympic Games and World Championships	• Evaluation of the results (depending on rank obtained) in significant competitions over the period 1996-1997 • Evolution of the results obtained between 1996-1997 and the period 1988-1989	Evaluation by the director for Olympic preparation (expert) for the Olympic federations and by the director of the office for elite sport of the Ministry of Youth and Sport for the non-Olympic NSFs

Table 6.7 **Examples of Economic and Financial Performance Indicators**

Variable to be measured	Indicator retained	Source of information
Capacity to manage the financial dependence regarding the help of the Ministry of Youth and Sport	Ratio of direct financial dependence on the Ministry of Youth and Sport/budget in 1997 Evolution of the ratio of dependence between 1989 and 1997	Reprocessing the information from the Ministry of Youth and Sport and federations' accounts
Capacity to obtain resources (and evolution)	Total financial results 1997/number of licensed athletes Evolution of total financial results compared with licensed athletes between 1989 and 1997 Number of State technical experts made available in 1997	Federations' accounts and Ministry of Youth and Sport
Capacity for investment and self-financing Financial health and balance	Ratio net situation/assets in 1996	Federations' accounts and Ministry of Youth and Sport
Capacity to generate resources within the federation's system	Capacity to generate grants from local authorities per licensed athlete, attributed to league committees and clubs	Study on the financing of sport by local authorities

performance by the societal contribution of the activities of each NSF using a single qualitative measurement: the degree of legitimacy attributed by an expert from the Ministry of Youth and Sport to the NSF's results and activities.

We can justify retaining only the opinion of an expert from the Ministry of Youth and Sport in order to evaluate societal performance by the fact that this body is a major or even predominant stakeholder for the NSFs. The Ministry of Youth and Sport is theoretically responsible for evaluating the pertinence of the response given to each NSF regarding the mission of public service entrusted to it by the State. We called upon the head of the office for single-sport federations, who was to rank each federation based on three variables evaluated at two different moments in time:

- The way in which the federation carried out its mission of public service
- The effectiveness of the way in which the ethical message (values, sporting spirit, etc.) was conveyed by the federation to its licensed athletes
- The social and economic impact of the federation's activities on society

In order to evaluate organisational performance, Bayle (1999) made a distinction between performance at a level of the federation's headquarters and that at a level of the federation's system.

Organisation performance was evaluated by the capacity of the structure of the federation's headquarters to respond, on an organisational level, to the expectations of its sponsors, of the Ministry of Youth and Sport, and the licensed athletes. The quality of information circulation between the various departments of the headquarters, the capacity of people within the federation to resolve technical problems (administrative, legal, information technology, etc.), the faculty of volunteer administrators to "get the federation's projects moving," and the global capacity of staff to carry out the tasks entrusted to them (but also within the various departments included in the administrative structure, etc.) were also retained to evaluate this performance.

The organisational performance of the federation's system was evaluated in terms of the quality of implementation of the federation's policy by area leagues and committees on a local level, as well as the clubs' capacity to respond to the demands of the licensed athletes on one hand and of those practising the sport on the other.

A total of 22 items were utilised for the performance of the federation's headquarters and 6 for the performance of the federation's system.

To measure the internal social performance, we asked the director to evaluate the social climate within the organisation. The term "social climate" is intended to qualify the conditions regarding the state of collaboration among salaried staff and among all players (volunteers, paid staff, and staff placed by the state at the disposal of the federation's headquarters).

Concerning promotional performance, the director was asked for a global judgment on the period 1992 to 1997 regarding

- the evolution of media coverage of the federation's disciplines (meaning the federation's image) and
- the impact of the federation's communication among its members (clubs and licensed athletes) and even among those practising the sport via all types of communication and promotion that the federation had available.

The image of the sport and its media coverage were evaluated by means of an objective indicator: the average of television hours broadcast between 1993 and 1997. Two subjective indicators and an objective indicator were retained for measuring promotional performance.

Finally, a total of 55 subjective and 10 objective indicators were utilised to evaluate the organisation's global performance.

The main limitation of our method lies in the fact that we were not able to obtain, for the 40 federations, objective indicators for three of the six dimensions of performance: organisational performance, internal social performance, and societal performance.

From the information described, we were able to pinpoint 65 measurement indicators for the 40 federations within our sample. These data were sufficiently extensive to allow us to draw up a typology of performance profiles.

Statistical Processing Methodology

The objective of the work by Bayle (1999) was to construct, on the basis of an essentially qualitative approach, performance indicators for the NSFs in order to establish a global performance measurement for each NSF and to highlight the existence of different performance profiles based on a typological approach.

Mintzberg (1986) reproaches researchers studying the relation between explanatory variables and effectiveness for the fact that their studies on contingency do not make it possible

to analyse the relationship in both directions. "Since most of these studies are of a synchronic nature (all measurements are carried out at the same time) and since the links between the variables are of a correlative nature, it is not possible to determine whether it is the contingency factors that are the cause . . . or whether causality takes places in the other direction."

We attempted to avoid this issue by carrying out a performance measurement over a 10-year period (1988-1997) for objective data and over a 5-year period (1992-1997) for the "subjective" data (evaluation by the director of the federation).

A performance score was established according to the average of indicators utilised for each dimension. Optimum performance can be visualised on a radar graph around seven axes (statutory performance was divided into its two main variables—elite performance and performance according to the number of licensed athletes—in order to study the correlations more accurately). The optimum performance consists of placing oneself as far as possible on each of the seven axes while having homogeneous scores as possible when seeking performance on each of the axes (see figure 6.3). Developing one type of performance to the detriment of others can in fact affect the global result and above all the potential performance: For example, weak organisational and social performances can explain the fact that economic and financial performance can degenerate over time.

The Six Performance Profiles

Six groups of federations were identified as a result of the statistical processing, using SPSS software. After analysis of the results from the scores, the averages, and the rankings for each performance, six denominations were adopted to describe the categories: "powerful," "effective," "dilemmas," "atypical," "deficient," and "problematic."

Class 1: Powerful

The category "powerful" includes five federations with homogeneous, high scores on all dimensions of performance. From a media point of view, these sports perform much better than the others. This is one of the main characteristics that distinguishes these federations from those in category 2. They are federations with the highest financial resources, and a priori perform well and effectively.

It should be noted, however, that the promotional performance attributed to the cycling and athletics federations comes from competitions organised outside of their control, and that the financial impact of these competitions does not create any direct profit for the federation. This explains a global performance and an economic and financial potential performance for these two individual sports that are much lower than for the three other sports.

Class 2: Effective

Here, the vast majority of federations are traditional Olympic federations, notably effective on an elite performance level and with a good level of societal performance. These federations, smaller than those in class 1, obtain relatively homogeneous, high scores on all dimensions but with a weakness on one or two dimensions of performance compared with the federations in category 1. The problematic dimension is essentially that of promotional performance or, more rarely, economic and financial performance (or both promotional and economic).

Class 3: Dilemmas

Federations in this group, Olympic and non-Olympic, often have two dimensions of performance that are rather unsatisfactory, with the others being average. The two problematic dimensions of performance are most frequently promotional performance and elite performance. In certain cases, the performance is very low (this is the case for shooting with respect to promotional performance).

Other federations have a globally average performance with weakness especially in organisational and internal social performance, or have average to weak elite and promotional performance results. This group of federations, whose size varies widely, are considered to be those with "dilemmas" since these federations do not appear to make sufficient use of their media, economic and financial potential, or base of practising athletes. They are federations that are undergoing major structuring or restructuring or that have encountered a specific problem.

Class 4: Atypical

This category includes federations whose performance is heterogeneous within the class and atypical compared with other performance profiles. They are not necessarily ineffective, but generally have performance clearly lower than the others. For the automobile and volleyball federations, this is elite performance, and for American football it is societal and elite performance. Boxing also has two major weaknesses: performance related to the number of licensed athletes and societal performance. This group is composed of federations with widely varying global performances (some were in the first quarter of the 40 federations on a global performance level and others were in the last quarter).

Class 5: Deficient

The four federations in this category appear to be encountering extremely serious problems. They have low scores on all dimensions of performance and a very low societal performance. Their financial situation is also highly precarious. The weightlifting federation, moreover, was legally liquidated in 1998 following the withdrawal of its ministerial certification.

Class 6: Problematic

The federations in class 6 are in difficulty in at least two dimensions of performance, notably economic and financial performance, because they are undergoing restructuring or are in a phase of strategic interrogation. For example, one federation has weak promotional, societal, economic, and financial performance. Another federation's economic and financial performance shows serious shortcomings and low societal performance owing to the evolution in the number of licensed athletes.

Certain federations, in contrast to others, are characterised by weak organisational and internal social performances. This statement should be interpreted with caution, however, because of the quality of the person responding and the particular contexts of internal political crisis.

In order to visualise the performance profiles, Bayle (1999) has drawn up radar graphs on the models in figure 6.3 with an example that characterises each of the six performance profiles revealed.

Class 1: Powerful

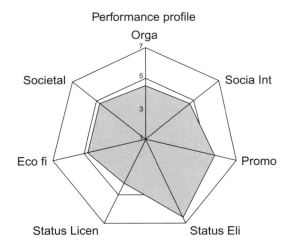

Class 2: Effective

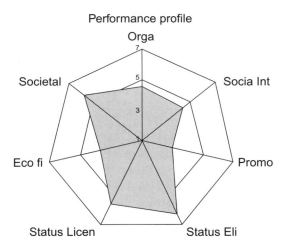

Class 3: Dilemmas

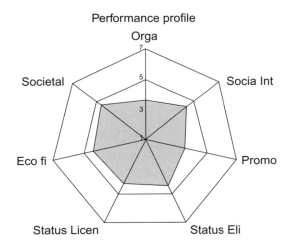

Class 4: Atypical

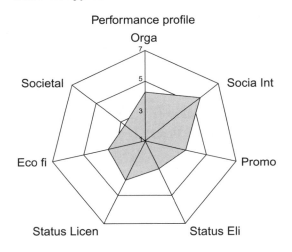

Class 5: Deficient

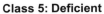
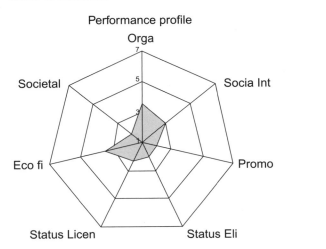

Class 6: Problematic

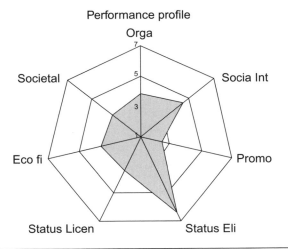

Figure 6.3 Radar graphs of the six performance profiles. Orga = organisational, Socia Int = internal social, Promo = promotional, Status Eli = results in high level competitions, Status Licen = number of members, and Eco fi = economic and financial.

The typology presented here gives a glimpse of the possible types of evolution in light of an analysis of the performance and actual context of certain federations. The method of measuring the global performance of the NSFs that we have proposed is based on the stakeholder theory of organisation. The typology presented appears to be richer and more global than one founded on economic and financial criteria, results on the elite or the number of licensed athletes (or a combination of these), or results for the Olympic elite alone. One advantage of the method is the possibility of aggregating the measurement of outputs in order to take into account the many dimensions of the performance of an organisation. A second advantage is that it allows one to place the performance of the NSF in comparison to other NSFs. Like all typologies, the one we have established has a reductive character, whether in relation to the indicators chosen or methodological limitations linked to the access to and processing of data and the choice of statistical processing.

Measuring the Performance of a Federation Over Time

Madella (1998) attempted to evaluate the performance of the Italian athletics federation (FIDAL) over time, based on a multidimensional approach that takes into account a maximum of pertinent criteria and indicators for the federation's stakeholders. In this perspective, performance is defined as the ability to acquire and properly process human, financial, and physical resources to achieve the goals of the organisation.

The criteria for measuring performance must be sensitive to the specificity of this kind of organisation and should reflect the whole input–process–output cycle and not just the end result (see figure 6.4). Performance criteria must reflect the interrelationships with the outside environment.

The basic phases for measuring and controlling performance adopted by Madella (1998) were as follows:

- Definition of the model (the global conceptual structure of the federation and the factors to be controlled). This model, with 11 dimensions, is mainly based on
  - perceptions of the organisational goals on the part of the stakeholders;
  - the content of reports and official documents (analysis of speeches); and
  - the resources and the capacities controlled by the organisation considered as the main antecedents for achieving goals—finances, human and tangible resources, other symbolic and organisational resources.
- Construction and validation of the indicators (110 in total) for each conceptual dimension
- Definition of the specific procedures for attributing values to the selected variables and identification of the sources of data and their reliability
- Determination of the weighting of the indicators
- Integration of the qualitative variables in the overall validation
- Validation of the system and the statistical model
- Collection of data and automatic report generation

The basic conceptual dimensions defined by Madella are these:

1. Finances
2. Human resources

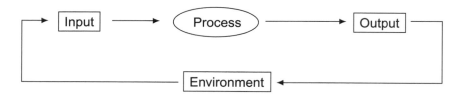

Figure 6.4 Input–process–output cycle.

3. Interorganisational relations
4. Athletes' performance (international level)
5. Athletes' performance (national level)
6. Quality of services
7. Production of events
8. Internal communication
9. Technology, logistics, and production factors
10. Production of knowledge
11. Flexibility and innovation

Table 6.8 presents some indicators linked to the dimensions of performance retained by Madella.

The author then determined a performance index for each dimension. The relative importance of each dimension was considered according to the weighting attributed by the stakeholders in order to construct a global annual performance index (see tables 6.9 and 6.10).

Madella (1998) proposes a more precise analysis of the factors of performance in gathering the dimensions and indicators. Input and environment factors allow better understanding of potential performance and the performance index of the federation (see table 6.11)

The methodology for measuring performance is richer than that discussed previously and makes it possible, based on the large number

Table 6.8 **Dimensions of Performance of the Italian Athletics Federation**

Dimension	Questions	Examples of indicators
Finances	Financial resources received Attribution of the various sources of financing (sponsor/State) Economic value/impact Operating costs Personnel costs	New sources of financing Alternative and traditional financing ratio Percentage of dependency on subsidies from Italian national Olympic committee Ratio of financing from households, State, local authorities, sponsors, and volunteer work Cost per member Cost per medal—cost for elite performance Personnel costs compared with budget Cost of staff (freelance/outsourced)
Human resources	(1) Participation of members in competitions Attractiveness for new arrivals Position among competition Turnover of members (2) Qualifications and competencies of human resources (judges, coaches, managers)	Number of members (athletes, judges, managers, coaches) Evolution of different categories of members Ratio of new members compared with total members Rate of renewal of the different categories Quality of coordination Courses available Level of qualification Percentage staff and employees working part-time and full-time
Inter-organisational relations	Penetration of the sport in schools	Number of pupils involved in athletics Number of school projects linked to athletics
Athletes' performance (international level)	Production of international results at elite level	Number of medals at World, European Championships, and Olympic Games Number of athletes in the top 100 and top 50 of each event Standing of the team at international competitions

(continued)

Table 6.8 *(continued)*

Dimension	Questions	Examples of indicators
Athletes' performance (national level)	Quality of performances in competition at national and regional level	Average performance of best, of best 10, 50, and 100 per event, sex, and category
Quality of services	Perception (subjective) of the quality of services—satisfaction of athletes, managers, judges, coaches Formal specification of quality of standards	Evaluation of the quality of services by the members (athletes, judges, etc.) by means of surveys and investigations Reference to quality in official speeches Number of facilities, clubs, coaches per 100,000 inhabitants Number of judges per competition Range of services proposed Types of membership possible
Production of events	Production of competitions and competition services	Number of competitive events organised by type of event
Organisational atmosphere and internal communication	Process of internal conflict and rate of conflicts	Number of meetings of management committees and other meetings Regularity of the information Disciplinary actions and controversies Quality of communication and information flow Negotiation process
Image and external communication	Public renown and impact and media coverage Interest on part of spectators	Measurement of image (by marketing surveys) Media coverage (television, press)
Logistics, technology, and production factors	Quality and adequacy of equipment	Quantity of equipment Condition and age of equipment Criteria for management Territorial distribution
Flexibility and innovation	Renovation of elite squads New forms of competition Organisational changes	New members elected at central and local level New events Average age of members of board of directors Ratio men/women on boards of directors
Knowledge	Cultural impact	Number of articles indexed to Sport Information Research Center

of indicators revealed, to pilot performance based in the selected areas. However, all the dimensions and performance indicators are not easily linked to the organisation's strategy in operational terms, and above all the evolution of certain indicators does not depend on the policy of the federation alone, but also on that of other actors in the environment.

Esposito and Madella (2003) have proposed an evolution of this model of performance-evaluation. According to the model proposed previously (1998), the objectives set by the federation have been distributed among seven main autonomous dimensions of performance:

1. Results obtained in international and national competitions

2. (Voluntary) human resources/clients (e.g., members, coaches)

3. Marketing and communication

4. Volume and quality of the services delivered to the users directly by the federation or indirectly by the affiliated clubs

5. Economic and financial performance

6. Internal process (including communication and technology)

7. Innovation and organisational learning

Table 6.9 **Raw Appraisal**

	1998	1999	2000
Finances	0.80	0.91	0.84
Human resources	0.96	0.99	0.99
Competition results (international)	0.81	0.78	0.82
Competition results (national)	0.83	0.90	0.91
Services	0.63	0.78	0.87
Events	1.00	0.98	0.98
Internal communication	0.76	0.75	0.93
Institutional commitment	0.69	0.82	0.99
Global Performance	6.48	6.92	7.33
Standardized Index	0.81	0.86	0.92

Table 6.10 **Weighted Appraisal (Based on Stakeholders' View)**

	1998	1999	2000
Finances	2.97	3.41	3.14
Human resources	3.87	3.99	3.98
Competition results (international)	3.69	3.52	3.71
Competition results (national)	2.22	2.43	2.46
Services	1.28	1.79	1.56
Events	3.10	3.04	3.04
Internal communication	2.28	2.25	2.80
Institutional commitment	2.16	2.55	2.08
Global Performance	21.57	22.78	23.97
Variation (%)		5%	4%

For each of these dimensions, specific indicators were selected, on which data were collected for the period 1998 to 2001, which corresponds to the reference four-year governance cycle

Table 6.11 **A Contingent Appraisal Performance**

	1998	1999	2000
Performance			
Index	21.58	22.78	23.97
Input	0.75	0.32	0.43
Environment	0.67	0.55	0.59

established by the Italian NOC for the NSFs. The indicators selected represent an update and substantial improvement to the list proposed and tested by Madella in 1998. The choice of the indicators for all the dimensions was made on the basis of the following criteria:

1. Review of the field-specific literature
2. Judgment of the stakeholders (collected through nonstructural interviews)
3. Viability of statistical analysis and treatment in relation to the typology of the different variables

The indicators that were chosen include two type of measures:

1. *Basic institutional indicators* (those immediately related to the mission that are usually stable and considered the essential core of NSF performance), for example, the number of members and coaches.

2. *Indicators of contingent priorities* specific to the period of time identified. For each dimension it is possible to build a single synthetic value through a specific calculation and standardization process that allows combination of the different indicators utilized. An identical process can also be carried out on the seven dimensions to allow the calculation of a unique and final performance index, whose validity is of course contingent on the chosen methodologies and dependent on the quality of the data collected.

The list of indicators was considered the most suitable to represent the set priorities, the nature of the organisations, and the limitations that can be foreseen in the short-term implementation of an assessment system.

The following techniques were used for the data collection:

1. Secondary statistical analysis of data produced by the federation in its administrative and statistical activity

2. Analysis of documents and official texts

3. Questionnaires administered to representatives of the different categories of stakeholders to assess their satisfaction concerning the effectiveness of the federation in the various key areas (the questionnaires are a modified version of an already utilised classical tool to investigate the perception of effectiveness developed by Chelladurai et al. [1987])

4. Interviews of key players (mainly to identify the real strategic priorities)

Data have usually been collected for the time period 1998 to 2001, but in some cases other data sets have been processed.

The raw data referring to all the indicators were treated and combined into a single index for each dimension, through a standardization process based on the highest value of each series (made equal to 1).

Since the organisational life of any Italian national sport federation (FIDAL) is based primarily on a four-year cycle, the authors mainly used the official reports presented by the president of the FIDAL and by the board of directors on the occasions of the three general assemblies of the federation carried out in the period 1997 to 2001. Through these documents and other text materials it was possible to access a systematic illustration and evaluation of the level of attainment of the set objectives after the first two years and at the end of the four-year period. This kind of communication, however, had more a political function than an integrated and balanced organisational control system, even if it included quite a large amount of quantitative information.

Through analysis of the official documents presented at the beginning of the four-year cycle and the interviews of the top executives and leading coaches of the federation, it was possible to generate a conceptual map of the strategic themes and priorities of the federation in the given period and associate them to a list of indicators. This methodological procedure (triangulation between official document and perspective of the actors) has been used to avoid taking for granted the official objective and to assist in identifying the "real" strategic objectives of the organisations that have resulted from ongoing negotiation between coalitions and groups of interests.

We present as an example the indicators chosen by the authors for the volume and quality of services, which make quite evident a general decline in the overall effectiveness of the federations in this area for both structural and contingent indicators (see tables 6.12 and 6.13).

Table 6.12 Core Indicators of the Volume and Quality of Services

Indicators	1998	1999	2000	2001
Number of clubs	2,917	2,859	2,841	2,833
Number of track and field facilities	914	937	945	966
Members per coach	22.2	22.9	23.7	23.6
Coaches' courses provided	29	18	23	20
Number of coaches attending courses	819	538	948	547
Anti-doping controls	926	639	838	633
Training camps	138	123	127	121
Number of total competitive events organized	5,748	5,509	5,672	5,420

Table 6.13 **Contingent Indicators of the Volume and Quality of Services**

Indicators	1998	1999	2000	2001
Number of voluntary managers attending				
Courses/seminars	48	937	945	966
Support to athletes				
Number of athletes involved	481	253	295	133
Support to coaches				
Number of coaches involved	182	47	112	78
Financial provisions to top-level athletes				
Medical care (millions of euros)	346	262	275	298
Financial support to athletes (millions of euros)	0.38	0.28	0.30	0.30

The overall evaluation of the trends of the FIDAL performance on the different dimensions is presented in table 6.14. The final results seem to indicate a much higher capacity to maintain a good level of performance on the basic core indicators than to produce substantial modification on the more contingent priorities. The average decrease in overall performance in fact is almost entirely accounted for by the contingent indicators. Another key issue is that some of these priorities are probably inserted into the strategic plans more with a political intention than a real capacity for or interest in their achievement. Greater involvement of the stakeholder in the process of selecting those priorities that really are incorporated within the federation policy is therefore advisable for the future.

Finally, the data referring to the different categories of indicators in relation to their position in the organisational system (input, output, throughput) have been taken into account. If we limit our attention to a very general analysis, it can be seen that in the four-year cycle many of the traditional input data such as those concerning financial resources and the number of employees and paid collaborators have decreased. The substantial stability of institutional performance and improvement in the input–output relation calculated on the pertinent indicators shows that a better throughput process has probably been implemented. Usually, this data are not available. In addition, there is usually an absence of qualitative judgment by the stakeholders and great changes in the principle of the accounting system that make it very difficult to develop a more detailed analysis of the efficiency of the system.

We have presented two perspectives for measuring performance of OSOs. These methods can both be used by managers of these organisations rather than by external consultants. As these approaches require reliable data, a specific process to collect, check, store, process,

Table 6.14 **Overall Evaluation of Performance of the Italian Athletics Federation (FIDAL)**

Overall performance of FIDAL	1998	1999	2000	2001
Performance on core indicators	0.91	0.83	0.83	0.83
Performance on contingent indicators	0.87	0.81	0.77	0.65
Overall raw performance	0.89	0.82	0.80	0.74

List of the Indicators Used in the System

Total Italian athletes in the world top 50 (men + women)

Medals won at top world international competitions (OG and WCs)

Finalists at top world international competitions (OG and WCs)

Ranking of the Italian team in the Europe Cup (men)

Ranking of the Italian team in the Europe Cup (women)

Number of athletes (women) in world top 50 IAAF

Ranking of the Italian men's senior team at the world cross country championship

Ranking of the Italian women's senior team at the world cross country championship

Ranking of the Italian men's junior team at the world cross country championship

Ranking of the Italian women's senior team at the world cross country championship

Position of the Italian men's senior team at the European cross country championship

Position of the Italian women's senior team at the European cross country championship

World indoor championship medals and finalists

European indoor championship medals and finalists

World junior championship medals and finalists

European junior championship medals and finalists

Position of the Italian junior men's team at the European cross country championship

Position of the Italian women's junior team at the European cross country championship

New national records (senior and junior categories)

New national records (youth)

Productivity index (men)

Productivity index (women)

Productivity index (overall)

New national women's records (all categories)

Size of membership (athletes)

Size of membership (coaches)

Size of membership (managers)

Size of membership (judges)

Young athletes

Master and amateur members

New coaches

Number of clubs

Number of track and field facilities

Members per coach

Coaches' courses provided

Number of coaches attending courses

Anti-doping controls

Training camps

Number of total competitive events organized

Number of voluntary managers attending courses/seminars

Support to athletes (number of athletes involved)

Support to coaches (number of coaches involved)

Financial provisions to top-level athletes (medical care) (millions euro)

Financial support to athletes (millions euro)

Income from sponsorships

World ranking of Golden Gala in IAAF events

Broadcast FIDAL events (in Italy) (number)

Advertising—TV rights

International events in Italy

Students involved in track and field

Income of the marketing initiative Casa Italia

Partners Casa Italia

Total turnover

Costs for technical activities

Investments

Operational costs

Percentage of budget from public subsidy (from CONI)

Subsidies from local communities

---

and interpret the data is necessary. An effective monitoring system for use in an organisation requires an adequate information system that allows quick and flexible input, retrieval, and treatment of information. FIDAL's next project is to propose a Web implementation of the database.

As Esposito (2002) notes, "to be effective, it is necessary that all the components of the organization at the different levels should be aware of the nature and use of the performance assessment system. Secondly, they should feel themselves involved through their everyday action in voluntary or professional work in the process of achieving some of the goals specified in the control system. Of course sometimes the relationship between the general criteria valid for the whole organization and specific positions can be very remote, weak or even conflictive. It is therefore useful that all the business units within an organization could develop their own specific monitoring tools, with clear relations with the overall performance criteria and indicators.

In order to develop the commitment by the constituents, a wide range of initiatives should be taken, that include the organisation of meetings and seminars at the central and local level with club and federation managers and professionals, the production of articles and leaflets, annual newsletters with performance data, and possibly a dedicated Intranet or extranet for the clubs. The attempt to develop the familiarity with the new tools, however, should not be occasional but based on a medium-term strategy. In particular, voluntary and professional managers should be able to understand the general methodology, the meaning and limitations of the different measures and the possibility to use the overall set of indicators or only part of them for their own specific purposes. A new incentive system for individuals, teams and groups should be developed with close connections with the performance assessment system and with a great attention to avoid excessive competition or even conflicts. Finally the connections between the performance assessment system and the existing reporting planning and control systems should be reflected upon to avoid overlap and contradiction."

In order to understand more fully the exact conditions for managing performance and to explain the performance profiles (Bayle 1999) or performance scores (Madella 1998; Esposito and Madella 2003), it is necessary to have a precise, if not intimate, knowledge of the organisation studied, taking into account not only the interaction of the individuals within it but also the interaction of the organisation with other organisations in its environment and beyond.

seven

Steering Performance of Olympic Sport Organisations

The problem of the Olympic sport organizations' (OSOs') development seems to be based on the following dilemma: that of modifying their strategic behaviour and organisational structures, or even their culture, without breaking apart and throwing into question their original identity, which is the basis of their legitimacy.

In the contextual framework of politics, economics, and social aspects that the OSOs have difficulty in affecting, we have sought to understand the fundamental mechanisms that could permit them to preserve or improve their performances (sport, organisational, financial, and others). In a doctoral thesis, Bayle (1999) carried out case studies on single-sport federations over a longitudinal period (mainly between 1988 and 1998) based on documentary sources, interviews, and on-site observations and using an analytical framework, adapted from Lawrence and Lorsch (1973) and specially established for the study of the OSOs' strategic and organisational behaviour (see appendix E). These case studies were conducted in OSOs of various sizes whose sports and financial performances differed greatly. The synthesis of these studies on the strategic and organisational behaviour of national sport federations (NSFs) (Bayle 1999) and other research work (Bayle and Camy 2003[1]; Thibault et al. 1991, 1993, 1994; Slack 1985; Slack et al. 1988) permits us to propose a general framework that will make it possible to understand the "strategic performance mix" determining OSOs' potential performance as discussed in the next section. With a view to this potential, the generic principles and methods that we call the "operational performance mix," that favour or restrict the performance of OSOs, are suggested (see section 7.2 later in this chapter).[2] Finally, the strategic performance mix and the operational performance mix must be analysed in a dynamic perspective, notably around the question of change and the adaptations necessary in managing performance as discussed in the final section of this chapter (7.3).

---

[1]Case studies were performed on five French NSFs to understand the activities and tasks managed by their main volunteer administrators concerning the organizational design of the federation.

[2]Each principle of operational performance was linked to the performance dimensions identified in chapter 6 by Bayle (1999), section "Performance Dimensions and Indicators."

7.1 The Strategic Performance Mix

Three major strategic principles on which the performance and potential performance of OSOs depend are as follows:

- The functioning conditions of the OSOs' governance
- The quality of the OSOs' networks
- The size of the economic channel and the positioning of the OSOs' systems within this channel

The Functioning Conditions of the OSOs' Governance

The complexity of management methods, strategic and organisational inertia, or even scleroses and conflicts noted by those analysing the OSOs (such as international and national sport federations) can be explained by the coexistence of two or three groups of actors whose status and interests are different or even at times opposed: the volunteers, the technical sport experts (for example, in France made available by the State for the NSF), and the salaried staff with a private law contract.

Within such a framework for functioning, taking decisions is an issue that is often impregnated by a powerful ideological filter (see on this subject Welch 1994 and the 1999 Special Issue of the *European Journal for Sport Management*). Moreover, associative decision-taking forms are part of a collective, and theoretically democratic, logic (general competencies of the general assembly regarding decision taking, of the executive committee for applying strategic decisions, and of the management team for daily management. This explains the slowness of the decision-taking circuits, sometimes accentuated by electoral concerns that limit strategic horizons to four-year Olympic cycles. This is particularly true in structures in which the issues at stake and power struggles are strongly present as in OSOs.

Our case studies, like analyses by some other authors (see Slack 1985), show that the system of governance and notably the permanence and position of the main volunteer administrators are among the keys to an organisation's

success. This conditions strategic reactivity and organisational adaptability, the desire to adapt to the environment, the constancy and permanence of management monitoring, the quality of collaboration, the methods for controlling salaried staff and technical experts, the performance criteria that are finally determined, and so on. The functioning of the system of governance seems clearly linked to contextual factors, but above all to the profile of the OSO's president. The president's (or sometimes the secretary general's or treasurer's) professional background and situation, as well as his or her personality, charisma, professional career, and career within the OSO's system, are decisive in explaining his or her

- choices regarding management methods (strategic directions, political functioning, relations with volunteers and salaried staff, recruitment policy, etc.);
- open-minded or hidebound approach to management tools (formalised or less formalised culture, encouragement or discouragement of delegation, etc.);
- position within the environment (areas of knowledge, competencies, personal contacts, networks, etc.), his or her legitimacy and aura within the federation's system; and
- desire to control decisions (centralised or decentralised power; delegation or no delegation of management of certain dossiers) in relation to the principal paid managers (national technical director, salaried directors, etc.) or volunteer administrators.

The actors associated with the development of an OSO's project construct a system of governance step by step. Analysed at a given moment, this system is only the result of a complex equilibrium that stems from the interaction of influences and power between all actors within the organisation (volunteers and paid staff). Case studies of OSOs reveal similarities but also differences, which permitted Bayle (2001) to define four main methods for governing international and national OSOs:

1. **"Strong presidency"**: The president takes the major decisions; he or she controls the functioning of the OSO and usually surrounds

him- or herself with two close colleagues to implement these decisions (usually the technical director and director of administration).

2. "Tandem presidency": In this form of governance, also termed the "president/director tandem"), the authority to take decisions is shared almost equally between the technical director and the president.

3. "Dispersed presidency": The president coordinates all the directors, thus positioning him- or herself in the situation of a director general.

4. "Managerial": A technical director or a salaried director controls decision taking, either formally or informally, and a great deal of confidence is placed in this person by the main volunteer administrators who tacitly accept his or her authority. One must understand the term "managerial" as referring to a form of governance that favours giving power to salaried staff over volunteer administrators.

According to the methods of governance, the voluntary board of directors has a role whose complexity varies. Notably in a participative system, as in the case of certain OSOs, it is possible for the board to play a quadruple role: "control, militant, tool and facade"—terms taken from Mayaux (1999) and explained as follows:

- The "board as a controlling body" actually leads the association and controls the work of the salaried staff. The board members are perceived as bosses playing their role as employers and sometimes exerting authority.

- The "board as a militant" means that the administrators are above all dedicated, committed militants. They feel they are the guarantors of the institution, of its philosophy, and of its ethics. The board of directors is perceived as a political body.

- The "board as a tool" gives advice and offers opinions and help. The board members are perceived by the salaried staff as colleagues and as supporting them. The board of directors is seen as a place for exchanges, reflection, and proposals, like a support group.

- The "board as a facade" corresponds to a system in which the role of the board of directors is extremely limited and formal. Board meetings often consist of ratifying decisions that have already been taken by the salaried staff.

The role of the board and the result of the "negotiation" procedure between volunteer administrators and paid staff reflect the relative power of each member within the dominant coalition, depending on the control of strategic resources, information, or specific competencies. The system of governance does not appear stable but remains more or less evolving. The case studies show that the forms of governance revealed are not necessarily pure, but rather mixed. They provide an idea of the existing methods of functioning and the current compromises of power and prerogatives among the main strategic actors of the federations.

The "strong" and "tandem" presidential regimes are more characteristic of OSOs whose administrative structure is still modest (generally less than 20 salaried administrative staff at the OSO's headquarters), whereas the "dispersed governance" and "managerial" regimes are related to managing more complex systems (over 50 salaried staff). It is evident that there is a cycle of evolution for these four types of governance, which would indicate that the equilibrium of power between volunteers and paid staff depends on the life cycle of the organisation.

The Impact of the Forms of Governance on Strategic and Organisational Functioning

Table 7.1 presents the characteristics of the four systems of governance within the OSOs. Charismatic governance can be a fifth type of governance that can map on one of the four governance types. The following table presents the impact of systems of governance on the strategic and organisational functioning with regard to a certain number of characteristics as outlined in the table.

It is difficult to determine whether one form of governance proves more effective (see Papadimitriou 1999) than others, but the various forms have varying degrees of fluidity and rapidity of decision taking. The method of management adopted seems to be linked to the personality of the actors but also to the context (political stability, stable/dynamic environment, favourable/ unfavourable environment, etc.).

Table 7.1   **Characteristics of the Systems of Governance of OSOs**

Characteristics of governance type	Strong presidency	Tandem presidency	Dispersed presidency	Managerial	Charismatic
Degree of centralisation of decisions	Very strong	Very strong	Strong but can be dispersed	Strong but may appear fairly participative	Strong
Internal method of control	Strong and direct, by the president	Strong and broken down formally or informally between the two actors	Depending on the directors' method of management	Depending on the director's method of management	Depending on the dominant actor's culture
Type of board of directors	Façade–tool	Façade	Façade-tool	Façade-control-tool	Militant-advice-tool
Key actors (in charge)	President	President, technical director, or administrative director	President	Director (general) or technical director	President
Culture and profile of key actor (*"doctrine"*)	"Company man" and ambitious person focused on project or actor who seizes sole power (*"Centralise to advance or control better"*)	Hybrid person ("political" or focus on synthesis); masters the intricacies of politics (*"Centralise to control power"*)	Hybrid person (political animal or focus on synthesis) (*"Divide to reign" = management of compromises*)	Technical and strategic competencies + holder (guardian) of the philosophy. (*"Manage to develop better"*)	Specific technical competencies and democratic legitimacy (*"The father paves the way, others follow naturally"*)
Management style	Authoritarian and coercive; coordination via the hierarchy; organisational rigidity; control of actors and results, all strategic decisions taken by the president.	Authoritarian and directive (hierarchy); decisions attributed according to areas of competence of two actors or decision taken dually on fundamental points.	Variable depending on president and directors; managerial delegation to directors, who report to the president who takes the final decision	Based on the culture and beliefs of the dominant actor; seeks effectiveness	Based on culture and beliefs; Seeks effectiveness
Presence	Permanent	Problematic if not permanent and not pertinent		Permanent	Permanent
Legitimacy of the actor	Very strong	Strong to medium	Weak to very weak	Very strong but expression of this varies	Very strong
Major advantages	Rhythm of innovation; rapidity of decision taking	Rapidity of decision taking	Response to various environments	Rhythm of innovation; rapidity of decision taking; permanence of role and mastery of key internal factors	Internal coherence and absence of conflicts; rhythm of innovation; rapidity of decision taking

Characteristics of governance type	Strong presidency	Tandem presidency	Dispersed presidency	Managerial	Charismatic
Disadvantages and/or major risks	Democratic legitimacy at question; deviation into autocratic power	Deviation into autocratic power; conflicts between the two (loss of confidence)	Need for varied and powerful integration mechanisms; risk of absence of command unit	Confidence in the director is modified; change in the balance of the power of unpaid staff	Departure and succession of the charismatic actor
Rhythm of decision taking and advancement of projects (legitimacy)	Rapid (political)	Rapid (political)	Slow and analytical (technical)	Political and technical	Rapid and almost always legitimate
Performance criteria favoured	Statutory; promotional; economic and financial; *focused on quantitative criteria* (number of licensed athletes, medals, etc.)	Focused on statutory (visible signs of success)	Plural; different or even diverging depending on actors	Statutory, organisational, internal social and external social	Statutory, promotional (social and media recognition)

The size of the organisation and of the headquarters (number of salaried staff and of directors, etc.), the desired rhythm for getting action and dossier moving, explicit and implicit performance criteria retained by the actors of the dominant coalition, and the president's desire to master decision taking are also crucial in explaining the method of management. It is clear that the professions and socioprofessional categories to which sport executives belong create very different visions of how an organisation should be led.

Several OSO experts highlight the fundamental resource consisting of the sociological basis of the volunteer administrators of a sport, notably at the club level, and their capacity to implement projects that are often proposed by the top management of the federation. In France, for example, the cycling and boxing federations have club executives whose psychosociological profiles are mainly those of shopkeepers or craftspersons, in contrast to golf, where the executives tend more to be upper management and heads of companies.

The various systems of governance show different balances of power. The presence of a counter-power to the dominant actors, generally the president, sometimes appears necessary in order to prevent the system from degenerating into autocracy. The term autocracy can be applied to the case of one person who wishes to personify communication from the given OSO or sport, to centralise all decisions, or in cases in which there is confusion between personal interests (political, media related, financial, etc.) and those of the federation.

Complex methods of governance require a strong internal and external legitimacy on the part of the dominant actor. Otherwise, there is the risk of politicisation and a sclerosis of the system to the advantage of political games that could lead the organisation toward a political arena resembling that described by Mintzberg (1986).

The time spent within the structure by the president who places him- or herself in the role of a director general or president—director general appears crucial only to the extent that a risk of absence of authority exists (blocking the decision-making process) and underground struggles take place to acquire or master authority. In such cases, the organisation runs the risk of functioning on performance criteria that are favourable to the dominant actors in the absence of the president (generally, one or several directors).

The presence and legitimacy of the president thus appear necessary and essential to forming the basis of effective, sustainable work. These elements explain the dynamic of certain OSOs by the frequency of coordination and exchange among the actors within the organisation. During a period of growth, in which the intensity and rhythm of work are high so that numerous projects can be handled, moments of coordination and concert appear essential in order to maintain a participative system. Informal coordination methods are fundamental. The coordination of the salaried staff sometimes takes place via the culture of conviviality alone. Such coordination, however, nevertheless appears fragile to the extent that it is more closely linked to places and people than to systems of management. Strong interpersonal relationships and common interests, notably among the salaried directors and the top managers, also constitute a powerful or even crucial method of informal coordination in organisations where political games can be present, particularly during election periods.

We have examined the forms or types of governance for the OSOs by showing that these are only rarely expressed in a pure form and that they are also subject to the phenomena of evolution and degeneration. Nevertheless, they constitute a fundamental component of the construction of strategic and organisational behaviour of the federations—revealed by the strategic unity of the federation, the rhythm and type of decision taking, and the favoured performance criteria.

Experience shows that the governance mechanisms often depend on the personality of the individuals, and notably of two to three main actors (not necessarily the president alone but also the technical director, who is a person with crucial authority in the OSOs, especially in France). The perversity of the traditional electoral system within OSOs, which function by indirect democracy, is also a major destabilising factor for managerial power.

This indicates that the decision-making outcomes of the OSOs' boards seem to be produced through political processes, which have significantly replaced any scientific, technical, professional, or rational procedures (see Bayle

2001 and Papadimitriou and Taylor 2000, for example).

We now propose several mechanisms aimed at facilitating the effectiveness of the OSOs' governance with a view to rendering volunteer administrators and salaried directors more motivated and willing to take responsibility, to play more democratic and accountable politics, and to create more internal and external transparency—reflecting those suggested by Asensi (2000), Bayle (2000), and Papadimitriou and Taylor (2000). These mechanisms are listed under two major categories: (1) ensuring diversity and minimum level of competence and (2) favouring control and transparency.

Ensure Diversity and Minimum Level of Competence

• Give the OSOs the possibility of choosing methods of governance that are sometimes more appropriate to the realities of their functioning by opting for systems of governance that are close to that of certain limited companies—executive board and supervisory board—representing, in this latter case, the interests of the stakeholders, for example, private companies present in the OSO's system.

• Reform the statutes of the OSOs by distributing votes among all the federation's stakeholders, that is, representatives of the clubs, regional leagues, and area committees but also coaches' unions, professional athletes, judges, and referees, in order to favour a democratic atmosphere.

• Give the OSO's president the possibility of being remunerated as is the case in certain international sport federations, but also introduce a limitation to the number of years as president. This possibility appears necessary in order to open up the functions of president to persons whose social and legal status could suffer from an unpaid position. In certain countries (such as France), the majority of presidents of NSFs or the national Olympic committees (NOCs) come from the civil service (and are sometimes made available by the State in order to practise their unpaid function) or are retired.

• Create specialist roles on the boards (medical doctors, lawyers, external and independent administrators, etc.) and design the selection procedures to fill them.

- Establish board manuals that outline the role and behaviour of the members and stipulate their participation and their active roles (mission checklist) in order to regain their motivation.

- Give participation opportunities on the board to stakeholders (athletes, sponsors, women[3] etc.) and paid staff (directors). This opportunity would make it possible to clarify authority regarding commitments and the prerogatives of salaried staff (notably the directors) in relation to volunteer administrators and external partners.

Favour Control and Transparency

- Permit concentration of the board's energy and experience on policy development issues, determining the mission of the organisation, establishing standards that ensure accomplishment of organisational objectives, and facilitating boundary activities.

- Favour the implementation of ethics and nomination commissions, such as the ones established by the International Olympic Committee (IOC) in 1999 following the Salt Lake scandal.

- Establish control committees. For example, offer the general assembly, the OSO's committee, or its external partners (a major sponsor, the Ministry of Youth and Sport) the possibility of designating an external auditor whose work will extend beyond that of the certified accountants and the usual auditors. An audit committee or an independent expert on the management of OSOs can also be used in case of tensions at an organisational level.

- Limit renewal for the OSO's president to two consecutive periods in office. This limitation appears necessary to avoid the personalisation of power in the OSO and prevent this post from becoming an issue of personal power. The perspective of the re-election process for presidents is an issue that often detrimentally influences the strategic and organisational functioning of the OSOs. In 2002, the IOC decided that its president could be re-elected only once for a four-year term following his or her first eight-year term. An age limit of 70 years was also established for new IOC members.

- Elect the OSO's president by a system of direct democracy, based on a programme, and expand the elective system to all components of the OSO's system and not to local organisations alone.

- The obligation of a president to present a detailed programme to all stakeholders would contribute toward transparency in relation to the members and would avoid the holding of an election on the sole basis of politics.

The mechanisms proposed are aimed at avoiding political sclerosis linked to the current elective system and "corporate governance" of the OSOs, and above all at clarifying the decision-taking process and encouraging an internal executive team to assume responsibility, for example toward external partners. Certain types of evolution can be imposed or can remain optional as a first stage, and concern only the international (or national) federation's or NOC's headquarters and not the leagues or area committees. The question is whether the sport system and the OSOs' volunteer administrators are ready to accept such changes from a cultural point of view. The analysis by Chifflet (1987, p. 293) is still highly topical: "The federations have rarely accepted those coming from other fields (unlike major industrial companies or banks, for instance) and constantly draw upon their future executives from their own sector. This is valid for volunteer administrators and for technical experts whose past within the federation is a more important reason for nomination than any other characteristic (qualifications, personality, interpersonal skills, professionalism, etc.)."

A second key point regarding OSOs' potential performance is based on their networking quality.

---

[3]We have to remember that the IOC recommended that NOCs have at minimum 10% of women members in their voluntary board of directors before the December 30, 2000, 20% in 2005 and 30% in the next ten years. If most of NOCS have created women specific commissions and programs to develop women sports leadership (thanks to the financial help of Olympic solidarity often completed with governemental subsidies), the requests of the IOC have not been respected by the NOCs. In France for example, the government has introduced in the sport law the principle of proportionality between the number of women members of the NSFs and number of places they have at their disposal in the voluntary board of directors of NSFs.

The Quality of OSO Networking

The phrase "quality of OSO networking" should be understood as the quality of the relations among the actors of the federation's network (international federation [IF], national federations, regional leagues, area committees, sport clubs) or the NOC's network (regional Olympic committee, area Olympic committee) on a level of reactivity, reliability, and the solidity of the links that unite the structures of the federation's system.

The primary task of a federation is to federate, in order to create solidarity between the units of which it is composed, in order that these do not compete among themselves. This solidarity must be forged while taking into account the three major zones of pressure (on a level of allocating prerogatives and financial relations among the organisations): IF/NSF, league/area committee, professional clubs/professional league/federation (see figure 7.1). In order for the system to function, social peace is essential (i.e., an absence of recurring political conflicts, the necessary transparency or at least the actors' sense that transparency exists) as is clear communication of the NSF's system toward the media, the public, and private actors.

At least two closely intermeshed strategies are used by the NSFs to improve the quality of their network: formal conventions among the organisations of the federation's system and seal of approval for clubs and commercial structures that provide sport services to licensed athletes or those practising the sport concerned.

This research into the quality of the networking within a federation can take the form of a system of conventions such as that practised today by some federations: a mandatory convention between the professional league and the NSF and between the NSF and its regional leagues, which provides the precise attribution of financial resources.

Managing an NSF must, in fact, be envisaged as a system that consists of various links in a chain. These links have different roles depending on the NSF's development project. The theoretical objective of the federation's project is to define the principles and conditions behind the functioning of its system. Formalising this project (see part I) for an NSF exerts an influence on the other components of the NSF's system that can make them aware of the necessity of adopting a strategic approach.

In almost all NSFs, the area committee is generally the weakest link within the federation's system and seems to have been neglected in terms of professionalization. It always falls outside the management of the system for issuing licenses, and administrative and financial relations operate mainly between the federation and its regional leagues. Within small or medium-sized federations, the objective of creating an area committee is to benefit public sources of support from the area in question (from the local authorities or the area's youth and sport service, etc.) that may be applicable, but its reason for existence is not specifically to improve the functioning of the federation; it even tends to make functioning more complex.

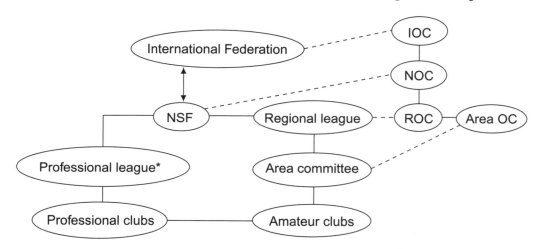

Figure 7.1 The national sport federation system. * = Within the European sport system, professional leagues are placed under the official supervision of the NSF.

In certain cases, the political existence of area committees is not necessarily the guarantee of effective functioning given the limited resources at their disposal and the counter-authorities that they may constitute to leagues, as is notably the case in the major federations (football, tennis, basketball, etc.). Cohesion and dialogue among the five links (including sometimes the professional league) in order to implement the development project appear essential, even though they are necessarily difficult to achieve given the political and legal autonomy of each. This network, traditionally presented in pyramid form, should today rather take the form of a network organisation (rapidity, flexibility, adaptability, reactivity, etc.)—a form that nevertheless is very difficult to implement. As Desbordes et al. note (1999, p. 347), "It is essential to put the federations' power regarding strategic direction into perspective. The federations' directives regarding services, communication or prices are rarely applied by all clubs, and the creation of new clubs to a large extent escapes national executives. At most, they attempt to channel local initiatives by proposing affiliation in exchange for grants. We are a long way from the perfect distribution network."

The objective of this latter is no longer to govern from the top downward via hierarchical relationships at each level of the system, but by means of a networking system based on contractual relations between all the federation's partners. The capacity of the federation's network as a whole to make use of the opportunities of the environment explains, for example, the success of some federations.

The French judo federation masters the system of 'bottom upward': The clubs work for the federation, and the latter works for the clubs. The key individual in the system appears to be the club's salaried coach, who brings in long-standing know-how and professionalism, which facilitates the application of the federation's sport and educational policy. The symbiosis between the five links in the system appears to be based on a political unity with shared values and a clear development project known to all. It operates, seen more simply, thanks to professionalism in structures that facilitate a more intensive rhythm of completing actions and the communication of information that facilitates adaptation strategies, even though all managing systems are faced with inertia due to the size of the federation's system.

The main difficulty concerning the federation's networking is that of the gap, of varying sizes, that may exist between the innovative capacity of the federation's headquarters and the system's aptitude for implementing these innovations. Here there is a risk of a break occurring between the head and the base of the federation's system. The entire issue, and the difficulty for the federations, lies in leading the regional and area committees (and the clubs) each to play their role in applying the federation's policy while helping them to assert themselves as local actors perfectly in tune with their environment and capable of acting upon it (making use of opportunities for financing, the capacity to collaborate and contract with other local actors and other private partners, etc.).

To take up this challenge, the federations are trying (notably under pressure from the State by means of subsidised contracts, State subsidies, a reduction in social charges, or a combination of these) to professionalize their system and the various links in the chain in order to improve communication and the implementation of their actions. Federations also implement intranet technology that allows a direct and constant flow of information in real time to and from their own local branches' structures (improvement of the information system in the national sport network).

These attempts may also include local partnerships negotiated and driven at a national level via a contractualisation approach between the federation and its noncentral structures or even its clubs, at times linking the attribution of resources and other forms of support to a certain number of conditions. The multiple relations with agencies within the federation's system are liable to lead to a dissemination of financial means. Leagues and committees may sometimes be veritable local potentates while constituting unavoidable relays for implementing and controlling the federation's policy. For this reason, more and more NSFs sign contracts regarding objectives with their own regional committees. These systems give the federation a tool that incites control and managing (knowing the conditions for applying the federation's plan, being better informed about the global—

financial and sport—situation of the leagues, orienting support according to needs, getting information from the field, i.e., from the club base, etc.). For example, one of the most original methods is the financial incentive mechanism implemented by a French sport federation with its regional committees concerning the management and production of licenses (freedom to fix the price of the licence and to keep the profit from licences above a certain amount).

Such a principle of formal conventions gives the leagues and regional committees the opportunity to formalise their action project within a perspective spanning several years. Since the rules of the game are submitted to all the leagues in advance, this permits more regular contact with the federation and a clarification of the methods of allocating the federation's aid, which can at times operate on a political basis.

This logic of development will be favoured by the professionalization of the federation's system, and via the system of formal conventions, which must allow decentralization of competencies to regional branches (with financial human and logistics support to implement national projects). It may at times bring about a far-reaching mutation of the culture of the sport in question, as well as a change in the methods of managing the associations that can be difficult for traditional clubs to integrate.

Case studies of NSFs reveal the necessity, in order to promote the quality of the NSF's network, of ensuring that the federations know and control local sport groups. This control aims to measure application of the federation's policy but above all to verify the quality of the "services" supplied and thus the capacity to achieve fidelity and growth in the number of licensed athletes. The quality of equipment and facilities (in terms of education, activities, etc.) within the clubs is an obvious fidelity vector. Strategies to create a seal of approval (permitting recognition of the quality of services and practices) initiated by the federations aim to improve and control the quality of services proposed by the clubs or other structures for those practising the given sport.

Local groups carry out self-assessments based on highly detailed grids of criteria relating to information from the person practising the sport (signage and facilities), structures (functioning, premises, equipment, sites, etc.), and the activities proposed. This self-assessment based on a logbook makes it possible to award three levels of seals of approval.

All the structures affiliated with these sport federations can, on demand, be given seals of quality if they satisfy a list of conditions including a certain number of quality criteria (Pigeassou and Chaze 1999, p. 35). The sailing, rowing, canoeing, and waterskiing federations distribute these seals of approval, the criteria used showing a strong heterogeneity (see Pigeassou and Chaze, p. 50, for a synthesis). In return for the investment and the commitment to quality made by affiliated clubs, the federations offer various types of technical support (promotional material, communications work, etc.) and sometimes financial support in order to encourage employment in this sector of activity. The seal of approval appears as the guarantee of a reliable organisation. It is an accelerator of promotional activity, a vector of external communication, and a federative and stabilising element within managerial behaviour. United by contractual links, all the partners fulfil a predetermined mission: The groups endeavour to respect the quality charter, controls are carried out by the area or regional committees, and the highest body supervises control and issues the seal. A logbook lists the club's material and human resources in order to establish an evaluation. Adding together all the structures that have received a seal of approval constitutes a relatively uniform, standardised network from a quality point of view. This seal-of-approval system could apply to other sports in which the cohabitation of commercial and associative structures is particularly frequent (tennis, squash, horseback riding, golf, etc.).

A sport federation wishing to approve and control the largest possible number of associative or commercial groups can favour communication around this concept of a seal of approval. Those who have obtained it must have significant promotion among a public informed of the quality and level of the sport facilities and services. The use of the federation's logo and image makes it possible for approved commercial structures to assert themselves and for clubs to achieve media coverage or financial support.

Given more unstable types of behaviour on the part of those practising leisure sport, the essential factor is for the beneficiary of the seal of approval or federal certification to be able to create fidelity among its adepts and to create a dynamic, evolving element of improving quality—and finally, to use a protected brand name and logo as distinctive signs of the federation issuing them for promotional purposes. The other element for justifying seals of approval concerns a better awareness of the structure, of its means, and of its results for local partners, permitting these latter to evaluate the reliability of possible collaboration with the federation's system, which is the guarantee of professionalism, effectiveness, and control of the product.

Behind the idea of a seal of quality, in fact, is the emergence of a system close to that of franchising by the federation that unifies and favours the development of the sports in question based on a more qualitative, uniform approach.

The general professionalization process of the system can favour the implementation of such an approach, although with the risk that a major cultural change within the associative movement will take place, among others. Some will see this is as the wrong direction for the associative movement to take and as a turn to merchandising, while others will see it as adapting to the constraints of today's environment. Such a perspective justifies the importance of a mutual stance regarding resources on the level of the federation's policy, notably in order that the financial mass stemming from the leisure activity remains with and mainly benefits the federation's activities.

Through offering a seal-of-approval system to clubs and commercial structures, a federation's ability to control the sport system can be greatly strengthened. This supposes a clearly defined, global strategic project on the part of the federation and one that is formalised and shared by its various components. Such an ambition implies a behavioural quality on the part of the main actors that induces generalised professionalism within the federation's system. This perspective could, however, increase differences within the federation's system and, more widely, could lead to a change in the associative culture.

Via these types of evolution, the most effective and most legitimate federations in the eyes of the local authorities appear to position themselves as organisations offering a maximum of services adapted to the needs of the organisations in the federation's system. The effectiveness of such a strategy can only work in the form of a "network organisation" that goes beyond the traditional pyramid structure of federations in order to react to demands on the part of local public or private partners (who are becoming increasingly demanding).

Beyond the quality of the federation's network and the joint work of the various components (club, league, committee, etc.), it appears that the OSOs with a big performance potential are those whose economic channel is the largest, but also and above all, those within which the OSO is best positioned.

Size of the Economic Channel and Positioning of the OSO's System Within the Channel

For hierarchical reasons, but also depending on the evolution of their strategic positioning, the federations occupy varying positions within the economic channels for their sport. The term "economic channel" should be understood in a broad sense: It means the economic wealth created within a specific sport sector (football, tennis, etc.) by equipment manufacturers, by the professional structures of professional educators that spread the sport's renown, organised sport events, and so on. The actors—at the origin of the creation of this economic wealth—can be both directly and indirectly public actors (State and local authorities), commercial (television, manufacturers of sporting goods and equipment, service companies for leisure sport, etc.), and associative (the federation's system: the clubs, the federation, elite sport, educators, etc.)

Synthesis of research into the federations' strategy (notably by Thibault et al. [1993, 1994]) plus research by Bayle (1999) allowed us to isolate seven factors that determine the size of the economic channel of a sport and the conditions for the federation's positioning within it.

• *The power of the sporting goods industries,* which can be analysed by the turnover of the sporting goods industries in the given sport (which determines the economic potential of a sport and a sport federation). All sports are not in equal situations regarding commercial development. Economic studies reveal that sports requiring considerable equipment (e.g., automobile sports, nautical sports) and costly individual sports (e.g., skiing, golf) benefit from a high commercial impact (and are thus greatly assisted by manufacturers) as opposed to sports practised in schools (e.g., handball, volleyball). This market for sport equipment makes it possible to evaluate the financial and economic interests that gravitate around the practice of a sport.

- *The commercial intensity surrounding the sport,* which varies according to season, according to the tourist-oriented and leisure aspect of the federation's sport (which determines the potential attractiveness of the sport).

- *The intensity of the professionalization of the teaching channel* and its relative location, that is, whether or not it falls within the associative services available (which determines the potential of technical professionalization).

- *The circuit(s) for spreading the sport* (e.g., municipal, in schools, in associations, commercial, or free practicing), which determine what is available on a more associative level (the case of judo), a mixed level (tennis and gymnastics), a municipal-based level (swimming), or a commercial level (canoeing and kayaking, horseback riding or squash). The configuration of the circuits for spreading the sport determines the potential of what is available (capacity of clubs in terms of members) and thus the intensity of the competition that the federation's system must face.

- *The density of the sport events* that are commercialised in the form of shows (potential for events). One can check events that belong to the federation's heritage to compare federations's events to the global event's economy in the sport manage by the federation.

- *The quantity and accessibility of the equipment necessary for this sport* (potential for the absorption of the sport).

- *The cost of the sport,* which comes from its characteristics (whether or not it requires apparatus or material) and other data, notably the circuits for spreading the sport and the accessibility of equipment necessary.

The concept of economic channel must be understood broadly. We must take into account voluntary work and other indirect resources (e.g., facilities disposal, lobbying capacity).

For example, Madella et al. (2000) assess at EUR 429 million the overall economic value of Italian athletics (size of the economic channel), encompassing all the economic activities directly and indirectly related to athletics such as services for travelling or health services and the global occupational impact, direct or indirect. With the voluntary work carried out by managers, judges, and trainers included, the overall economic value would be EUR 669 million.

These seven interlinked factors determine a combination of strategic resources that favour the given sports to varying degrees and that explain the national or international federation's central or peripheral positioning within the sport's economic channel. They affect, in fact, its potential performance. Here, it is worthwhile examining more carefully two points that appear to be key factors for determining the positioning and evolution of the federation within its economic channel:

- Does organising sport shows, with paid tickets, benefit the federation directly (i.e., by increasing its resources)?
- Does the OSO benefit directly, from a financial point of view, from the leisure activities that exist in the given sport?

Concerning the first point, organising sport shows, which usually constitute the main revenue for the large federations, we must make a distinction between collective and individual sports. For collective sports, clubs—via the professional league—constitute the essential link for any economic transaction. Here, the federation's system possesses a vital entrance barrier, at least in Europe (see the examples in Europe of football, basketball, and rugby). For individual sports, the same does not apply. The direct impact for the federation is usually less, because it is the athlete and not the club that is the essential economic link within any transaction.

Private organisers, for historical reasons or those of opportunity, can gain control of the organisation of the most lucrative competitions (usually at an international level), forcing out the national federal organisations (in the case of track and field or boxing, for example). But these latter competitions may be less important from a media and financial point of view than specific competitions (in the case of cycling with the Tour de France, for example). For this reason, federations such as those for cycling or boxing must be content to remain basically "collectors of tax and duties" from private organisers. At a limit, these organisations depend mainly on duties paid: membership fees from clubs, licences, subsidies from the Ministry of Youth and Sport, and organisational taxes on competitions. They do not benefit financially from organisation of the most lucrative competitions. The federation holds the position of a satellite within the economic channel. At best, it plays the role of an internal/external regulator of the economic channel, notably at an administrative and legal level. The financial impact of the economic activities of the given sport remains minor for the financing of the federation's activities. For these federations, the elite sector constitutes more of a financial burden than a major, essential product (in contrast to the cases of rugby and football). For this reason, gaining control of the organisation of lucrative events within the federation's system is more complex for individual sports than for collective sports and for the image of these federations.

Concerning the second point, few sports control a leisure channel that must pass via the federation's system. Elements such as the danger aspect, the complexity of the places and conditions for practice (material), and the necessary regulation of the sport may explain the varying degrees of federation control that is present with respect to these leisure activities. It is clear that sports such as cycling or swimming cannot control their leisure aspect as is possible, for example, for federations such as canoeing and kayaking, or to a lesser extent the sport climbing federation. The development of temporary licences to integrate the leisure market, as most federations are beginning to do, commits them to an approach that can at times be seen in a poor light by clubs because of the tax impact this implies. Sailing, waterskiing, and golf clubs, as well as equestrian centres and other structures offering activities in response to a seasonal demand, clearly experience this problem.

In France, for example, because of its strategy regarding events, the French tennis federation (organiser of the Roland Garros and Bercy tournaments) appears to be in a central position within this system, as is judo, although its economic channel is much weaker. Hiking is another major actor here, but weightlifting is a modest satellite beyond its vast and dynamic fitness sector. Gymnastics, with the explosion of the fitness market in the 1980s and 1990s, has been attempting to reposition toward the centre of its channel since the mid-1990s, notably with niche areas such as events and training.

The French basketball federation has been caught up in the economic and media wake of professional basketball in the United States, whose commercial, worldwide strategy has, however, limited the French federation margins for action since the beginning of the 1990s. The specific feature of the strategic situation of basketball in France and in Europe is the world impact of a foreign—or more precisely American—championship with its own rules of play that differ from those in Europe, as well as an image that has become popular throughout the world, competing on an economic and media coverage level with the other championships. This context does not exist in any other sport. For this reason, unity between professional basketball and leisure basketball within the federation is extremely difficult to achieve.

The approach of opening up to other publics appears essential in order to position a sport at the centre of its economic channel (and further political and social channel). This applies to tennis, with the organisation of the Roland Garros and Bercy tournaments for the benefit of the federation's system. The most characteristic example of a deficient positioning by a federation is that of the French ski federation. This has clearly remained apart from the flourishing economic system that skiing experienced in the 1980s, although the French Ropeways Company and the French ski school drew full benefit from that system. For this reason, the French ski federation appears as a modest satellite of the major French economic channel of skiing.

The more central the position of a national or international federation appears within its economic channel (the size of the economic channel is another key element), the more the federation's system can benefit from the financial impact in order to develop its coaching activities for the elite athletes, to implement a service approach to its members, and, more globally, to engage in diversification projects.

83

The federation's potential and profile will thus vary depending on the size of the economic channel for the given sport and its positioning—central or otherwise—within this channel. This positioning determines the federation's contractual capacity and the interest, or virtually the obligation, on the part of the stakeholders to act in partnership with it. The federation's position within the economic channel of the sport will also determine the interest of both public and private partners and thus the capacity to obtain resources for its system. Further, most federations try to become the sole and legitimate discussion partner of private and public actors of their sport's economic, political, and social channel.

The quality of a federation's network and the importance of the economic channel of the given sport mean increasing the federation's contractual capacity. This means the adoption of a formalised project with clearly identified missions and objectives, but also, and above all, generalising alliance and cooperation strategies that will take on a more legitimate role than the traditional, competitive strategies adopted in the world of business.

The three factors that we present make it possible to define the OSO strategic performance mix, which will help us understand the performance potential of an OSO (see figure 7.2).

The principles and methods of managing internal adjustment on a strategic, organisational, and control level also constitute the principles and methods that may prove to be obstacles or vectors regarding performance.

7.2 The Operational Performance Mix

The varying potential and the performance profiles depend on specific integrating mechanisms, some of which are performance vectors (key factors of success of operational performance) while others are constraints (key factors of failure) to achieving performance that are generically found in OSOs.

Key Factors of Success of Operational Performance

Within the OSOs are three main generic mechanisms that constitute key success factors of operational performance:

- Professionalization under the control of volunteer administrators
- Organisational culture as an essential participative mechanism
- Quality of partnership relations, and more generally the approach of services offered to internal and external stakeholders

OSO STRATEGIC PERFORMANCE MIX

Governance	Network quality	Economic channel
Principles		
Decision and control processes Define strategic vision, mission, and objectives Establish evaluation and control	Capacity of the OSO's system to deliver services Capacity of the OSO's network organisations to work together	Capacity to directly or indirectly generate resources (financial, logistics...)
Tools		
Strategic planning Power distribution Evaluation system	Conventions for objectives Seal of approval Professionalization/training	Determine size of economic channel and OSO's position within it Try to position OSO in the center of its economic channel

Figure 7.2 Diagram of the three strategic performance mix factors.

Professionalization

Professionalization (the technical management of dossiers and the actions delegated to permanent staff: salaried staff, staff made available by the State, or volunteers with time and specific competencies) under the control of volunteer administrators is a vector for progressing with and implementing projects. It requires, however, a clear allocation of work and of prerogatives between volunteers and paid staff. Beyond this, as Madella (2001) and Slack (2001) suggest, the role played by professionals can be to launch the organisation into "de-institutionalisation," notably of the voluntary values, by favouring the recruitment of volunteer administrators whose profiles correspond to those of heads of companies and innovators.

This approach can belong to the culture of sport executives in the OSO (respect for know-how and the status of individuals; notably in martial arts federations). It can be explained by the private resources generated and the culture of its leader(s) (deliberate determination to structure the OSO by recruiting qualified administrative and commercial staff of a high level), justifying a strong differentiation that makes it possible to respond to the expectations of the environment. The operational management (implementation of resource management) carried out by permanent, qualified staff results in an increase of specialisation, although paradoxically, the power to take decisions remains in the hands of volunteers (Madella 2001). It makes better knowledge and control of dossiers possible, which favours more effective, pertinent decision taking by volunteer administrators.

This early approach of professionalization and of know-how regarding training for elite athletes was driven in France by the State at the beginning of the 1960s with the creation of a unit of State technicians made available to the federations (approximately 1,700 experts). Via their methods of organisation, the French sport federations were progressively able to capitalise on specific areas of know-how alongside more traditional areas (training of the elite athletes by organising championships, management of licences, etc.): a quality training system for the French judo federation; a profitable event approach for the French tennis federation (economic development of Roland Garros at the end of the 1970s and the beginning of the 1980s) to

the benefit of the federation's system; the commercial development of a publishing sector (the maps/guides for the hiking federation in the 1980s); an event approach for the French gymnastics federation initiated by its main partner, France Télécom (1990s). Level and forms of professionalization can be very different with respect to the role (political, managerial, or operational) played by volunteer and paid staff (Bayle and Camy 2003).

It is possible to distinguish three "pure" roles and three mixed roles for volunteer administrators as follows.

- *"Purely political"*: The volunteer administrator is centred on managing the OSO's strategy, taking decisions, assuming institutional representation, lobbying, and controlling the achievement of objectives. He or she belongs to the executive committee and delegates to permanent staff (paid or not paid) the operational management tasks.

- *"Purely managerial"*: The volunteer administrator manages and is responsible for a specific programme or project or department. He or she coordinates a team (of paid staff, volunteers, or both) and takes the main decisions to steer projects (e.g., recruiting, affecting resources). He or she is doing the work of a paid staff director.

- *"Purely operational"*: The volunteer administrator assumes operational tasks: specific and highly qualified tasks (law, data processing, health care, marketing) or less qualified tasks (e.g., administrative, reception).

- *"Political and managerial"*: The volunteer administrator is more in the position of a general director who coordinates the work of managers and staff. He or she manages the recruiting and functioning of the different departments of the headquarters. This positioning is often deliberately arranged to avoid giving the power of mastering the system to a paid staff manager. The physical absence of this volunteer administrator (generally the president) gives rise to the problem of a lack of power and coordination.

- *"Political and operational"*: The volunteer administrator performs operational tasks in addition to his or her political tasks. This situation can be explained by the fact that volunteers have specific competencies in a field (e.g., communication, marketing, law, data processing) or must assume these duties due to the lack of paid staff. One can find this organizational context in small OSOs.

- *"Political-operational manager"*: The volunteer administrator has or wants to play several roles in the OSO to control the structure. Such a case poses no problem in small organisations but brings about difficulties in more complex and bigger OSOs.

The frontier between political, managerial, and operational tasks is difficult to identify. It is very seldom that members of the voluntary board of directors play only a purely political role. Most assume managerial or operational tasks or both.

The number and the role of paid staff and volunteers allow identification of three organisational forms in the steering of OSOs (Bayle and Camy 2003):

- A *"clear differentiation of status and roles."* Volunteer administrators assume a "political" role, and technical and administrative staff assume managerial and operational tasks under the control of volunteer administrators.

- A *"relative undifferentiation of status."* Paid staff take part in political decisions with a "differentiation of roles"; managerial and operational tasks are assumed by paid staff.

- An *"undifferentiation of status and an undifferentiation of roles."* The operational tasks are also assumed by volunteer administrators and volunteers.

This analysis framework allows us to understand dynamics of OSOs' professionalization (structure, activities, individuals).

Levels and forms of professionalization appear to follow a cycle in four stages.

Stage 1: *"The first restructuring"*

This stage marks the first administrative recruitment process in the following areas: secretarial staff, accountants, and those in charge of the administrative handling of licences or even the organisation of championships. Strategic functioning is based on volunteer administrators, with a sport policy defined together with the technical experts (national trainers) made available by the State. This first stage is characterised by a low level of delegation to permanent administrative staff and by a balance of power that is highly favourable to the volunteer administrators or even also to the State technical experts compared to the salaried administrative staff.

Salaried staff at the federation's headquarters number between 5 and 10. These numbers must be interpreted more as a tendency that is foreseen than as clear, incontestable, and verified figures that represent reality. An administration manager is not always present, but the technical director can pilot the entire OSO via a function that is in fact that of a director general.

Some specific tasks that cannot be carried out by volunteers and paid staff are sometimes externalised to specialist service providers (e.g., communication and marketing agencies, law and accountancy consultancies). Volunteers (in the executive board, in the supervisory board, and in commissions) have to assume managerial and operational tasks (e.g., administrative, communication, marketing) to enable the functioning of the federation (in relation to the absence or the lack of executive paid staff).

Stage 2: *"Functional specialisation"*

Stage 2 is characterised by the recruitment of specialists in communication and partnership (at stage 1, this work was most often outsourced to a specialised communication and marketing agency), in law, in information technology, in organising events, and the like, and of sport experts under private law contract (at headquarters or on a regional level). Certain functions can be outsourced, even if study of the strategy of the OSO tends to reveal a move toward self-organisation rather than outsourcing functions. This second stage reveals that the paid administrative staff, through the specialisation of functions, are becoming in many cases important advisors to the volunteer administrators. It marks the first managerial delegation of management and can bring with it a partitioning between the sport and administrative sectors. The salaried staff present at the federation's headquarters number between 15 and 40. An administrative manager or even a director is usually present, even if the national technical director, depending on his or her personality, can also assume the overall coordination. The arrival of managers (sometimes unpaid and volunteer) holding highly specialised functions brings more complexity into relations with the volunteer administrators who in the past coordinated or even handled these tasks.

According to the OSO's resources, functional specialisation can be assumed in some countries by technical managers (who are sometimes made available by the State) who do not have specific competencies to assume such tasks. This is why they have to be trained to assume new tasks (e.g., technical experts perform functions of development director, marketing and communication director, event director, or general director).

The president or the dominant actor has a key role in managing the compromises of power that are necessary between the director(s) and main volunteer administrators.

Stage 3: *"The coordinators"*

This stage marks the recruitment of project managers at a headquarters level, an increase in the level of support staff, and the hiring of marketing experts and management and coordination staff, or even external consultants being used for strategic management (assistance in formalising the development project or the marketing and communications policy).

Recruitment is also stepped up on the level of the leagues, with posts for secretaries or even those responsible for administration, in part financed by the federation, and posts for coaches or technical experts under private law contracts at a regional level. This third stage shows that the ratio of power between volunteers and paid staff can become inverted in favour of the salaried staff, to the point where volunteer administrators feel dispossessed of the federation's management and the decision-making process. This stage is one of changes, balances, and compromises of power between unpaid staff/technical experts and administrative paid staff. The number of salaried administrative staff at the federation's headquarters is over 50; several departmental directors are present, and sometimes a general director coordinates the whole. The role of the volunteer administrators is more focused on strategic management and control and less on operational tasks delegated to paid staff.

Stage 4: *Virtual generalisation of "professionalization" within the OSO's system*

The differentiated structure continues to increase with the appearance of the notion of departmental heads and directors (increase in the levels of support staff). This stage also corresponds to professionalization beginning to take place virtually throughout the OSO's system, from the club level with the presence of salaried coaching staff but also in administration. The development of activities and the intensity of the professionalization of the headquarters and the OSO's system modify the level of differentiation and integration, and justify the implementation of new methods of coordination. The number of salaried staff at the federation's headquarters is now above 100; the regional leagues have between 5 and 10 permanent employees. The area committees also begin structuring themselves around some permanent, nonmanagement staff and coaching specialists. This stage can represent a far-reaching transformation in the associative culture because of the intensity of the professionalization.

The relations between professionalization and performance are described in figure 7.3.

Figure 7.3 Relationships between professionalisation and performance.

One of the consequences of the professionalization of an OSO's structure is a natural tendency by salaried staff, notably managers, to justify the specific nature of their roles by adopting tools or management methods that stem from their experience in companies or their knowledge: for example, adopting the principle of written employment contracts, introducing an incentive system and the features of management by objective, systems of multiple coordination and concert, definition of the status of the staff, principles of organising work hierarchically.

Volunteer administrators may often feel that incentive mechanisms "go without saying" and that salaried staff are "remarkably fortunate" to work within the OSO. There may be a gap between the perception of the volunteer administratorsand the real motivations of the paid staff that the salaried director can bring to light.

Paid staff often attempt to make volunteer administrators aware of and familiar with

- needs regarding formalisation (strategic plan, information system, awareness of the environment, working relations, etc.) that mark reflection on strategic and management control;
- the necessity of introducing incentive schemes (salary increases, reflection on the status of salaried, on the conditions for progressing within the structure, on the training possibilities for staff, etc.), which expresses an initial reflection on human resource management;
- the gap between legal functioning and the legal constraints that are valid (necessity to comply with fiscal, labour, disciplinary, and European law, etc.), which shows a first analysis of the legal management of the structure; and
- implementation of specific actions intended to improve effectiveness and efficiency (reflection on the type and measurement of performance).

The structuring of the organisation may thus appear as a performance in itself (better services to the licensed athletes and clubs, event approach, search for sponsors) but one that is not legitimate unless it serves to achieve improvement with respect to other issues (statutory performance).

Finally, the complexity and technical aspects of management problems give salaried management staff and those in highly specialised functions (legal, financial, etc.) a legitimacy justifying the strengthening of their status in the eyes of the volunteer administrators. Their work frees the volunteer administrators from operational tasks that at times they may not master well in order to permit them, in theory, to concentrate on work of a more strategic nature (the organisation's project, taking decisions, etc.) or of a political kind (representation, lobbying, etc.).

The legitimacy of the salaried staff seems even stronger when the competencies they master are essential for the development or the functioning of the structure and not known to or mastered by the volunteer administrators. For example, during a phase of conflicts or uncertainties regarding regulations, the legal sector benefits from this legitimacy. The quality of the information system for the management of licences and championships (computer systems) is a major priority during the organisational phase. Marketing also becomes a major priority during phases of markety uncertainty and to know what practising athletes need.

This, moreover, is why some volunteer administrators (or even, in certain cases, paid managers and, notably, a national technical director deeply rooted within the structure) look for volunteer to take responsibility in their area of professional competence so that the structure can benefit from their know-how (or from their professional networks in the case of lobbying work) and also to avoid dependency of the structure on the salaried staff. Technical knowledge of the subject allows volunteer administrators to carry out work on a dual level that is more effective (based on knowledge of constraints linked to the task, etc. In France, this desire appears to be highly developed in judo and in hiking, where the volunteer administrators are often familiar with the principles and conditions for managing a company because they have done so in the past (upper management or heads of companies). The democratic legitimacy of the volunteer administrators also comes from their technical legitimacy and the know-how they have developed in their professional life.

The Organisational Culture

Managing an OSO during a period of growth is often characterised by a participative system. This system is based on involvement and personal commitment, where the feeling of belonging to and identifying with the organisational goals is strong among volunteers or even among paid staff. This involvement can be characterised by three factors: a strong belief in and acceptance of the goals or values of the organisation (or both), the desire to make considerable effort for the organisation, and a very strong intention to continue belonging to the organisation. This participative system may evolve into a more entrepreneurial management system that requires the management staff to assume more responsibility, notably via their association with the definition and implementation of the OSO's strategy and the control of their departments.

This initial evolution toward participative-type management was developed during the 1990s and the 2000s in certain OSOs; but the mechanisms were pushed much further by some federations and NOCs with the participation of all management staff in the executive committees, the implementation of an incentive system for the staff, and high levels of remuneration for managers (mechanisms similar to those found in large companies).

Analysis of the participative mechanisms within associations reveals forms of mixed commitment on the part of the salaried staff, notably managers, who may well have non-pecuniary objectives: taking part in a sport or human "adventure," preserving a sport, building a financial and cultural legacy, or seeing it bear fruit. These motivations can explain the intensity of work and the time devoted to the structure (often more than 60 hours per week). The feeling of belonging to the "family" of the OSO can also explain the involvement of the actors (which can at times also be analysed as attempts to court volunteer administrators).

But today, OSOs pay more attention to the "recruitment" of their volunteers and take into account competencies developed in the volunteers' professional lives and the time volunteers can offer the OSO. This is why they have to be more and more *"volunteer-professional"* (Bayle and Camy 2003). Control of the managers' work is mainly based on taking the initiative to assume responsibility, which, given the multiple involvement mechanisms, may seem relatively effective. However, in order to be legitimate, a person with responsibility must not only have the managerial and operational competencies linked to his or her function, but also share the value system of the sport and of the volunteer administrators, which justifies the confidence placed in him or her and the incentive to decentralise the operational management of dossiers to salaried staff. He or she has to be a *"professional-volunteer"* (Bayle and Camy 2003). It is, moreover, not surprising that the initial recruitment of salaried administrative managers in many OSOs is of former volunteer administrators from the headquarters or "regional levels" of the OSO.

The dominant actor, notably a president or a charismatic director, usually stimulates ambition and a development project justifying the scale of his or her involvement and the recognition of this by others. The fundamental role of leadership regarding cultural change is truly essential in such a context. We note that in certain countries, the presidents of OSOs have become professionals or businesspersons and that upper management of companies have been nominated as general directors of federations (in the case of Canada) in order to drive the change.

Driven and influenced by a strong leader, the closely working volunteer collaborators and paid staff find themselves in a kind of "psychological imprisonment." In extreme cases, a dominant leader may cause people to place the organisation's cause before their own life, believing this behavoir is justified and natural. However, as Mahé de Boislandelle (1998, p. 366) reveals, when managing small companies "the exercise of power by the executive can often take on an autocratic character which is accepted to varying degrees; it can also be combined with charisma if the staff admire him and have great confidence in him. Inversely, he may be accepted or rejected on the surface only, and create situations of rupture or resistance. In all cases, the situation of dependence by the staff, accepted or suffered, is very high" (Mahé de Boislandelle 1998,). The feeling of belonging to a "family" or a "team" can explain the actors' investment in a system that they contribute toward creating. Here, we once again find the mechanisms and principles revealed by research into psychology, notably those from the "theory of involvement" (Jacquelin 1992), according to which the actors imprison themselves via their psychological investment.

The role of the president or (director) appears to be truly capital here, since it can entail managing compromises of collaboration among salaried and unpaid managerial staff. The president will be able to preserve the organisational culture or associate salaried staff with the organisational culture. Avoiding politics within the salaried/volunteer relationship appears essential to preserving the internal social and organisational performance. The quality of collaboration between salaried and unpaid staff characterises the dual functioning that has taken place in some federations. The expression of the quality of this collaboration is that of confidence, the quality of the relation among the actors, and from their involvement in defining and implementing the actions of the development project.

For example, the development projects of the French canoeing federation for 1998 to 2002 and 2002 to 2012 were drawn up by a working group of about 20 persons (paid staff and volunteer from the clubs, branches and headquarters of the federation). The individuals were chosen for their interest in development.

The relation between organisational culture and performance is described in figure 7.4.

Quality of Service Approach and Partnership Relations

The quality of services and partnership relations, beyond the satisfaction of the stakeholders, appears to be an essential operational performance factor. This implies, first, that the OSO network has the capacity to carry out these services and partnerships (see "The Quality of Olympic Sport Organization Networking" earlier in the chapter). Secondly, it implies that the OSO's volunteer administrators should be capable of perceiving these expectations—that, for example, they have an information system that can reveal the expectations, categorise them, and place them in a hierarchy. This necessity is especially salient when the organisation's environment becomes particularly complex, turbulent, and uncertain. The OSOs are service organisations *par excellence and they must demonstrate the capacity of an innovation to satisfy stakeholders' expectations.*

The quality of service approach and partnership relations must be managed at three levels: services to OSO members, services to internal stakeholders, and services to external stakeholders.

• *Services to members* (i.e., clubs and licensed members and high-level athletes for an NSF; NSFs for an NOC; NSFs for an IF). Providing services to the members of an OSO can reinforce the network's quality and the legitimacy of the OSO.

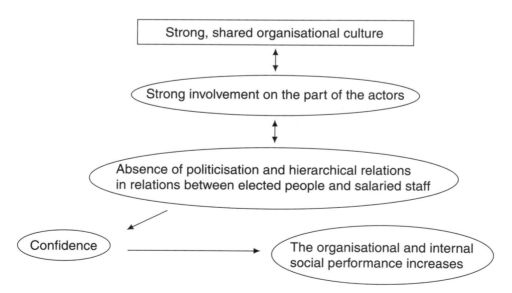

Figure 7.4 Relationship between organisational culture and performance.

The member service approach takes place more widely under pressure by the competition and given the risk that resources will become scarcer. Such practices as offering seals of approval (ranking and distinction of clubs related to a federal seal of approval defined according to the number of members, sport results or facilities, and the system's capacity for members, etc.) to clubs, counter-services to licensed athletes (partner clubs granting various advantages when taking out a licence), and services to clubs (e.g., NSF headquarters can create a specific department to assist club development in the fields of sport technique, law, economic data, and development advice) are implemented and justified in order to preserve an environment that in part has been escaping the control of the NSFs. The OSO's Web site can provide information to clubs and athletes: database, structure roles and competencies, calendars of competitions, rules, classifications, information for members, photos and videos of competitions, information on the management of a sport association. Services to elite athletes become more and more diversified: medical, financial, technical, retraining to promote high-level performance in sport and also the success of the athletes in their social and professional life after elite sport.

The best examples of the financing of application of this approach, in two highly different contexts, are French tennis with Roland Garros (the system of financing the development of services to the members of the federation) and the French judo federation for its marketing, development, and practise policy as applied to a specific target group of children aged 7 to 14 (with a high-quality system link to a social and sport project for the children). These strategic elements for differentiating services also usually benefit from a progressively consolidated, professional organisation that increases know-how and favours the phenomenon of organisational apprenticeship.

However, innovative strategies such as the organisation of international events can bring with them not only opportunities for media coverage and commercial aspects, but also risks linked to finances and image. Small, badly structured federations that are highly dependent on the State and that do not benefit from know-how regarding major events can experience financial difficulties following the organisation of international events for which resource management was not sufficiently mastered. Problems may include inability to control costs and lack of legal knowledge regarding organisation to avoid financial risks linked to the nonexecution of contracts. Such examples demonstrate that the strategic approach must be associated with and adapted to the opportunities and threats of the environment.

Organising a repeated event that can engender loyalty, and that can become a regular event within the national sport heritage, appears to be a vector for acquiring know-how, for satisfying stakeholders, and for multiple performance: promotional, economic, and financial (favouring the results of the national elite athletes); organisational (acquiring know-how); and internal social (increasing cohesion and exchange and highlighting the talents of internal actors around an event that will bear fruit).

- *Services to internal stakeholders* (regional leagues and area for an NSF; area Olympic committees, regional Olympic committees for an NOC). See "The Quality of Olympic Sport Organization Networking" on p. 78).

- *Services to external stakeholders* (other federations: NSFs, IFs, State, sponsors, TV). Services to external partners reinforce legitimacy and build partner loyalty.

A strategy of multiple formal conventions favours the acquisition of know-how in developing services. For an NSF, formal conventions within the sport sector appear to need to operate on several levels, all closely interlinked:

- *Vertical partnerships,* that is, of the federation with its noncentral bodies and its clubs (see network quality)

- *Horizontal partnerships* with other single-sport and multisport federations, with which strategic and financial synergies for development appear possible

The NSFs can also benefit from formal, horizontal conventions with the other single- and multisport NSFs if they have interests in common. This is notably the case for sports that use the same natural environment (water, mountains), the same sites or equipment (gymnasiums), or the same equipment supplier. At the end of the 1990s, two councils (superior council for water sports and superior council for outdoor sports) were created under the aegis of the French NOC. These councils have the aim of lobbying and proposing joint actions (e.g., training, equipment) to promote and develop these sports. Sports practised in a gymnasium (e.g., volleyball, handball, basketball) have taken a concerted approach, on the initiative of the Ministry of Youth and Sport, in order to unify the precise conditions for official certification of the sport halls and to draw up a reference document that permits local authorities to plan and more effectively study the concept of gymnasiums.

Most federations have reinforced their fading partnerships with schools and are involving the young generations (thanks to new formal agreements and conventions with national bodies charged with promoting school sport).

Similarly, and within the framework of a strategy involving greater solidarity within the sport movement, the NOC can also play a genuine role as a service provider toward the federations. These latter could decide, with a view to effectiveness and concentration of resources, to outsource functions such as legal matters (e.g., conflict management, consulting, training for executives or volunteers within the framework of the Olympic Academy). They could adopt common marketing and communications strategies, pooling resources at the level of information systems for marketing and accounting or managing derivative products, or launch joint media awareness campaigns. However, solidarity within the sport movement still appears somewhat low with regard to bringing about such a perspective, even though the activities of the NOC are showing a tendency for diversification. The French NOC has, since 1997, carried out several communications campaigns among the general public in order to promote the practice of sport in clubs (see www.CNOSF.org).

Even as competing bodies, it is in the interests of these federations to come to agreements in order to strengthen their negotiating power or their lobbying (among local authorities, as a notable example), their ability to achieve joint projects or initiatives (promotion, purchase of equipment, etc.). The perspective of such a cartel process, however, brings uncertainty with it as well as risks concerning the law on competition.

Within the NSFs, relations of cooperation do exist but often appear to be insufficiently developed. These relations concern practices such as information exchange (e.g., via a public interest group for Olympic preparation, information on the quality of service providers), reflection and action regarding a common future (within the framework of the French NOC, making it possible to define the strategy to adopt toward the public authorities), concert related to problems of seeking financial resources, and the like. If within charitable organisations cooperative and collective approaches take place because of a basic necessity, in the case of the NSFs the logic of mutual assistance and solidarity is clearly far less present.

For an NSF or NOC this lack of solidarity implies a systemic partnership with the body responsible for federating the federations in certain countries, the Ministry of Sport, and sponsors and private partners.

For example, the system of conventions for objectives that has been implemented since 1985 in France by the Ministry of Youth and Sport made it possible to impose clearly defined management and performance standards on the organisation (by laying the foundations of analytical accounting and budgetary analysis, etc.). Conventions implicitly incite strategic planning and rationalisation in order to introduce objective measurements for the success of the NSFs' policies. It would seem, moreover, that in the future the Ministry of Youth and Sport will reinforce its controlling role by making the allocation of resources conditional upon producing the appropriate controlling and evaluation tools. One of the wishes of the management for federations within the Ministry of Youth and Sport is to set up functional accounting that clearly reveals the attribution of charges and revenues per sector of activity. There is a commitment to set up analytical accounting features in the clauses of the convention regarding objectives, but to date, this measure has no legal basis. In this sense, it would be opportune for the Ministry of Youth and Sport to make it mandatory for NSFs to institute a simple internal control body in charge of drawing up a periodic overview of expenses versus budget, in order to guarantee the regularity of the operations carried out by the federation.

All the strategies involving multiple conventions that we have mentioned have the purpose of revealing the conditions for collaboration between an OSO and its partners. They have a favourable impact in the sense of improving the performance of the OSO (improvement in partnership relations and more widely in the approach of services offered to the internal and external stakeholders of these organisations). The only disadvantage concerns the agency cost linked to control over how these contracts are executed: creation and follow-up of logbooks, management control, and the like.

Often, and in addition to the Ministry of Sport, public companies are acting as the first major partners for sports that enjoy little media coverage. The approach by these companies seems to be partly that of patronage in an initial stage (despite major or even extraordinarily stringent contractual demands by these companies, there is a relative flexibility in implementation of the contracts). This first partnership generally goes hand in hand with a feeling of dependence and of fear on the part of the federation that this partner will disappear. It often triggers awareness and a desire to manage the dependence that involves looking for new partnerships, proposing new services to the main partner, or both. Unlike State financing, often considered by the federations' volunteer administrators as "going without saying," the arrival of a first, major private partner thus generates an indisputable dynamism regarding strategic reflection, internal structuring, and attempts to highlight the OSO's activities.

The OSO positions itself as a partner and a service provider.

Moreover, the formalisation that accompanies the method of monitoring the contractual relations (setting up contracts and conventions) can constitute a double-edged weapon. The non-formalisation of relations and the actual counterservices offered by an OSO to its partners can at times allow it to obtain more resources by letting a strategic ambiguity reign over its method of functioning, over the actual media impact of its activities, and over the reality of the unity that exists within the federation movement. Paradoxically, the organisation must in fact reduce this ambiguity internally and produce it outside the organisation (toward public partners, sponsors, broadcasters). This does not mean that the organisation does not seek to satisfy its stakeholders, rather that the organisation is seeking to keep them from interpreting it as weakness of the organisation. There is a compromise here that is for the OSO to define and handle internally.

The approach on the part of the federations to satisfying and rendering service to stakeholders and members is not necessarily proactive, but most frequently reactive. This reactive or passive type of culture can be explained by the considerable degree of financial dependence on the Ministry of Youth and Sport by certain NSFs. The federation is not necessarily an actor in the change; this is notably the case for federations whose media impact is still low.

The relationship between services to licensed athletes and performance is described in figure 7.5.

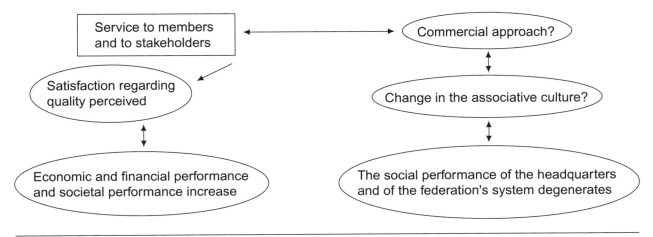

Figure 7.5 Relationship between services to licensed athletes and performance.

More generally, the link between the quality of partnership relations and the service approach to internal and external stakeholders and performance is described in figure 7.6.

The three key success factors of operational performance identified earlier in the chapter (see "Key Factors of Success of Operational Performance") are interlinked (see table 7.2). Organisational culture is clearly influenced by the levels and forms of an OSO's professionalization. The implementation of partnerships and services depends on the capacity to follow contracts and conventions. This is strongly linked to an OSO's professionalization.

These three factors and mechanisms, thus presented, appear incontestably as key success factors (to develop performance potential), although on the condition that they operate properly. If not, they will be added to all the other centripetal forms that may be encountered, to varying degrees, in any OSO-type body.

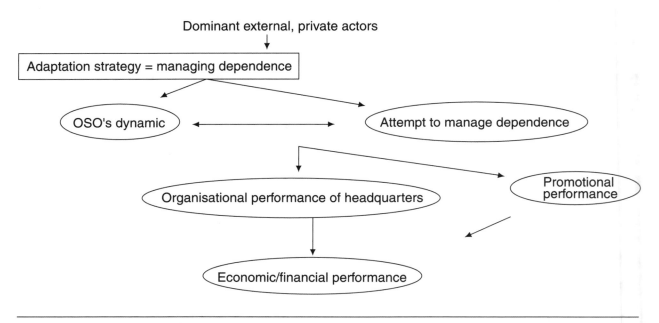

Figure 7.6 Link between performance and the quality of partnership relations and the service approach.

Table 7.2 **Three Interlinked Key Success Factors**

Professionalisation	Organisational culture	Partnerships and services
Principles		
Capacity to realize projects and tasks defined in the strategic plan	Involvement and cohesion around the OSO's strategy; working together (without conflicts)	Capacity for partnership (legitimacy); providing services to stakeholders
Tools		
Level and forms of professionalization adapted to OSO's life cycle and strategic planning	Respect for history, myths, values; recruitment of "volunteer-professionals" and "professional-volunteers"; team building, social climate	Delivering services regarding stakeholders' expectations; developing vertical, horizontal, and systemic partnerships through conventions and contracts

Key Failure Factors

Generally speaking, there are four types of constraints to integrative management (key failure factors):

- Nonexistent or deficient information and reporting systems
- Complexity of incentive mechanisms
- Deficiency or absence of control over the actors
- Political sclerosis present at the headquarters, in the OSO's system, or both

Deficient Information and Reporting Systems

Olympic sport organizations generally have a weak qualitative knowledge of the market and its evolution. Implementing a pertinent strategic and marketing approach can come up against a lack of qualitative information. Here there is an evident contradiction between the determination to adapt to the environment, or the desire to investigate adapting to it, and the poverty of the information system. The increased need for information and for understanding decisive issues within sport practice mainly emerged during the 1990s within the context of intensifying competition in three areas: competition regarding potential licensed athletes, the search for private financing, and access to the media.

Market and competition studies, however, are still little used. The fact that such tools are not used may perhaps be explained by lack of knowledge on the part of volunteer administrators, but also by a generally conservative organisational culture.

Efforts to collect external information on the profile of those practising a sport (quantity and types of practice) and their expectations, and the degree of satisfaction on the part of NSF: regional leagues and area committees, clubs, and licensed athletes, often remain extremely modest or nonexistent, as do concrete measurements of an OSO's renown and image and studies of the competition between various OSOs' activities. The quantitative and qualitative information on the environment is necessary to adjust the strategic and marketing policies. However, appropriate times and opportunities for collecting information appear numerous:

when licenses are being taken out, during general assemblies of leagues and committees, through mail shots to clubs, in the federation's magazine, and on the federation's Internet site or within Internet federations, for example.

The inward-looking, nonformalising culture is also seen in relation to defining the content of development plans (even if important changes have appeared in the 2000s). Introducing an effective external information system is nevertheless necessary for service organisations. This corresponds to four strategic and marketing issues:

- Defining opportunity and constraint factors linked to developing the practice of the sport (performance potential)
- A better knowledge of licensed and practising members of the public, which permits the implementation of a strategy for segmenting the public and thus the services proposed to the public
- Implementing a more targeted strategy toward partners (sponsors) depending on the socioprofessional profiles and types of consumption by those practising the sport (sale or use of the member list according to profile, joint commercialisation with partner companies of products or services among those practising the sport, etc.)
- An institutional form of communication that is more precise and pertinent for the local authorities and noncentralised bodies of the Ministry of Sport that often finance local development projects

It is not surprising that the pioneering and innovative OSOs with regard to defining an information system are those that are better structured and professionalized. Awareness and recognition of the necessity of external information collection mainly come from the need to explain a trend reversal for a drop in the number of those practising the sport or holding licences (tennis), stagnation in the number of clubs (see the example of studies implemented by the NSFs given by Desbordes et al. [1999]), or both. This type of study or survey can, moreover, be carried out via synergies with external partners to the federations and at times on the initiative of these latter, which makes it possible to reduce the cost of information for the NSFs, the Ministry of Youth and Sport, the Agency for Tourist Services, the National Tourism Observatory, the sport industries concerned, and so on.

One can presume that some OSOs do not know their environment well or at least not with sufficient precision (insufficient knowledge of their competitors, markets, and results and of the satisfaction of their stakeholders). Such knowledge, however, is one of the vectors of performance. It is for this reason, moreover, that according to some authors the core of the organisation is the information system, whose pertinence permits drawing up the strategic project and the marketing approach with a coherence.

The contradiction between growth in the complexity of the environment and the intensification of competition and of the rhythm of change in the sport sector on the one hand, and the poverty of the OSOs' external information systems on the other, reveals that the strategic approach, if it exists as such, is globally established on a highly intuitive basis. However, a better system is becoming more and more inevitable, and reflections concerning the methods and tools to be implemented are, by necessity, beginning to emerge.

The problem of the OSOs and the sport system in general stems from the fact that considerable quantitative information, often important, does exist but there is a genuine lack of qualitative information on the evolution of types of practise. However, the quality of the information available is a powerful factor in determining the quality of decision taking. The principle of a satisfaction survey among clubs, licensed athletes, and partners is not realised. Here we can follow the reasoning by Boyer and Charrier (1993, p. 622): "The probable evolution during the years 1990-2000 of a process of maturing within the sports system falls within a progressive rationalisation movement that began in the 1980s." The issue, as these authors stress, is to "professionalize decision-taking behaviour" on the part of both the actors (sport movement, etc.) and institutional partners.

We can use the expression "institutional short-sightedness" to express the idea that the organisation has an information system related to a perception process (vision) and that this can be deficient (short-sighted).

The OSOs studied seem to follow the same cycles of needs and priorities as companies regarding information systems. Historically, information systems for commercial companies began with accounting and budget management; few took into account information of a commercial and technical kind. For this reason, it is in many cases necessary to repudiate the concept of an information system for the OSOs.

Melèze (1995, p. 153) indicates that it is necessary to substitute the notion of data for that of information: "What is being built are data systems (quantitative and that can be codified: accounting, budget, technical, commercial, etc.) and that neglect qualitative, informal, and more abstract information."

In addition to this lack of pertinence and completeness of data for managing is the problem of how the data should be interpreted. Not all the information has an impact on the organisation's volunteer administrators—only the portion that qualifies as stimulating and that, integrated and understood, leads to decisive acts of effectively implemented managing and produces effects concerning the strategic objectives.

The deficient relation between the information and reporting system and performance is depicted in figure 7.7.

The internal communication system also proves to be one of the weaker links in the OSOs. The problem of bad horizontal information circulation at a headquarters level recurs. The phenomenon of lack of circulation or poor circulation of strategic information (e.g., mission, objectives to achieve) can be linked to power games between the actors. In any organisation, the individual who has power is the one who has information and distils it; the president or the director (or both) is often the best placed for this since he or she is at the crossroads of all information flows. Managing pertinent information is, for this person, a real source of power with respect to becoming well anchored within the structure. The strategy for consolidating one's power can explain the (desired) complexity of internal information circulation leading to an asymmetry of information between the president or director and the other actors.

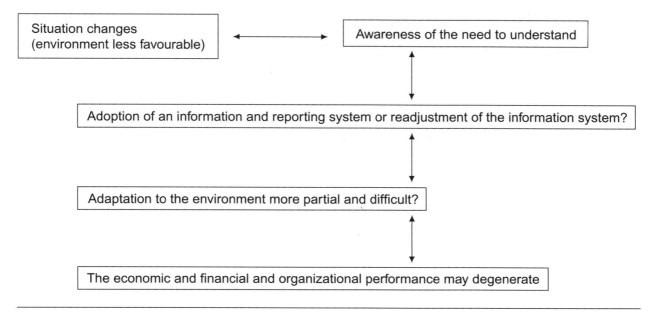

Figure 7.7 Deficient relationship between performance and reporting system.

The weakness of internal information between departments at a headquarters level can also lead to complexity during movement from informal communication management between the actors to the necessary formalisation of internal communication given the growth in size of the organisation (some OSOs' budgets and numbers of paid staff in Europe showed a 300% increase between 1993 and 2003). This growth in the organisation's size appears to be a common problem that must be managed by any developing small or medium enterprise. During periods of growth, quantitative information appears to be favoured, although this leads to a risk that the actors will become saturated in terms of their level and need for information. The actors can also operate an arbitration system based on the ratio of time investment necessary to construct and decode information systems versus improving the quality of information, which can be unfavourable to the structure, notably in a strong growth period. Crossing a certain number of organisational thresholds leads to the use of different management tools.

The relations revealed can be described as follows (see figure 7.8):

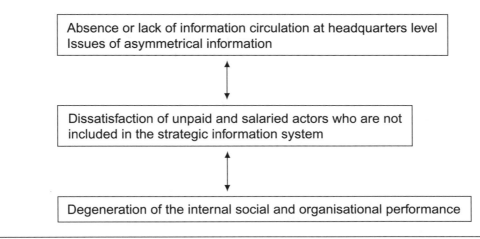

Figure 7.8 Deficient information distribution chain of events.

The logic of public service and that of associative service have long been invoked for the purpose of rejecting tools such as those of strategic and marketing approaches, that would mark the move to a managerial and commercial logic. These tools bring with them the idea of segmentation, classification, evaluation, control, or even sanctions, which is contrary to the unitarian ideology of the sport movement. The self-justificatory and ideological speeches by volunteers are a sign of a phenomenon of resistance to change and a fear of the unknown.

This situation poses a problem, since the failure to perceive pertinent variables constitutes a threat to the organisation to the extent that the gap that forms between the organisation and its environment can provoke a crisis of adaptation. The slowness to change or refusal to accept change can thus be explained by the complexity of the incentive mechanisms present in the management of the OSO's system.

The Complexity of the Incentive Mechanisms

In management, defining mechanisms of incentives for the external and internal stakeholders to cooperate in achieving objectives is essential for the success of an organisation. The OSOs do not escape this rule and depend on it completely with respect to development and performance.

On an internal level, the specific nature of the associative world comes from the complexity and diversity of incentive mechanisms that can be both pecuniary and nonpecuniary. These methods differ greatly according to the actors involved: unpaid staff/technical experts and salaried staff. In the associative sport system, the methods of involving these two categories of actors and the types of links they form are very different from or even opposite to those found in the commercial and public sectors.

The attention paid to incentive mechanisms of a pecuniary nature, notably those related to the social and salaried status of staff, is generally much less than in companies. This can be explained by the size of the NSFs and is the case generally for OSOs (the great majority of which are SMEs [Small and medium enterprises]), whether for cultural reasons or because of failure to perceive the issues behind the use of such tools. The associative world often appears less attentive to this aspect and favours a family-type culture.

It appears that incentive mechanisms are financial for salaried staff when their system of values seems to be somewhat out of harmony with the given sports and when the organisational culture is low or diffuse. Inversely, the nonpecuniary incentive mechanisms (pleasure, desire to give something back to sport and to serve it, etc.) can be much greater in the case of a culture close to that of the volunteer administrators. Managing the salaried human resources is, at best, envisaged at a level of the salary paid and the working conditions proposed. The question of an evolution in status and placing value on the work of the salaried personnel seems to be very little considered; similarly, staff training is not often provided. The practice of holding an annual evaluation meeting with each member of the salaried staff is not generalised. A profit-sharing system for salaried staff is not used and is judged to be of little worth or even inappropriate and complicated to set up in such organisations.

More globally, human resources management and the question of incentive mechanisms do not seem to be taken into account to any significant degree, and do not form part of the managerial culture of the OSOs because of their size (human resources management often represents a negligible function in SMEs) and the functioning of associative culture (for many volunteer administrators, the major involvement of the actors is viewed as a natural, or intangible, issue: "You have to be a 'professional-volunteer'.").

It is worthy of note that the salaried administrative staff, notably at the operational level, are in most cases not those who practise the sport of the OSO. This does not necessarily mean a lower level of involvement and a lesser degree of effectiveness in their work, but indicates that the value system and expectations of these persons do not function in a fundamentally different way than for the staff in public administration or in a company. Seeking security and professional stability, remuneration, progression as a result of the quality of work, a convivial working atmosphere, and so on can predominate despite the particularly unusual working conditions within the world of the federations: no commercial pressure, political-type relations with volunteer administrators, evaluation of work based on subjective and at times unclear criteria. The convivial atmosphere, the absence of commercial pressure and of the need to be profitable, and less stringent control all constitute the specific nature of the associative sector in terms of working conditions or even human relations. In contrast, however, the volume of working hours and hours of presence, notably for management staff (working during evenings and weekends), the forms of financial reward, and the relations with volunteer administrators are sometimes not well appreciated by the salaried staff in the absence of a collective convention or a company-type agreement that takes these specific aspects into consideration. A collective convention for sport is currently in preparation in France and social dialogue begins to emerge in Europe.

The politicisation of the OSO's system may concern the salaried staff, who are at times underground actors behind change or political stability. Close colleagues of the president, notably, can sometimes acquire a political dimension that is often superior to their official status. Pujol (1996), on the basis of an analysis of the functioning of large institutionalised associations such as OSOs, shows that the presence of interfaces between the various elements of the organisation gives secretaries and personal assistants a power that goes beyond their status. They control access to various persons, and beyond this can also exert a strong influence on the dominant actors (president, secretary general, and directors).

The extent of the prerogatives of the salaried staff and their future within the OSO often appear to be linked to recognition for their competencies and their complicity with the president and other "dominant" volunteer administrators. Instead of serving the organisation's vocation, salaried staff and notably those at manager level can seek to satisfy personal objectives (such as re-election) on the part of the dominant actor, generally the president, in order to strengthen their legitimacy. Their advisory role is aimed at anchoring themselves; their capacity to say no to volunteer administrators is reduced, making volunteer administrators aware of the strategic and organisational difficulties. The types of reward for the actors to maintain or strengthen their involvement remains a question mark in this type of organisation.

In all the OSOs, the evaluation system for administrative staff seems difficult to formalise and justify. Most important OSOs have tried to develop this practice without success and have more or less abandoned it. The remuneration–evaluation relation can consequently operate on an intuitive, or at times political, basis (proximity and fidelity of the salaried staff toward the dominant actor). For volunteers, the incentive mechanisms are specific and are generally based on social recognition for their unpaid investment. Usually, relational work, various advantages, and an attempt to achieve proximity exist in order to maintain the motivation of unpaid staff, notably the members of the voluntary board of directors, even if the advantages agreed upon can be seen as political "carrots" that are dangled in order to maintain the stability of the governance system.

The feeling of belonging to the structure on the part of unpaid staff is sometimes so strong that there is a risk that volunteer administrators will consider themselves indispensable, to the point of personifying the structure.

The joint bonding factor of incentive and cohesion among unpaid actors takes many forms. For example, in French OSOs, incentive mechanisms for unpaid staff can be based on a number of factors:

- A strong culture of serving clearly affirmed values that are a priori shared ("sport family")

- Political unity (presence of all the presidents of the metropolitan leagues on the voluntary board of directors for a better application of the directives for which they voted on a regional level)

- A growth phase around a charismatic leader and more globally a know-how system delegated to permanent (volunteer and paid) staff, multiple consultations, and major involvement of the volunteer administrators on the management team in strategic decisions

- Strong social recognition for the volunteer administrators on the voluntary board of directors (social image). It is legitimate to think that the lower the socioprofessional status of the volunteer administrators, the more the function of an OSO's voluntary board of directors (that of a president, above all, but also of vice presidents, secretary general, and treasurer) is regarded as image enhancing (as a stepping-stone in one's profession, as a way to increase one's network of relations, as a means of satisfying personal ambition, etc.), notably in OSOs that attract strong media attention and those that are powerful.

Incentive mechanisms must be taken into account in the management of the OSO's headquarters but also in the network's system (see earlier section on network quality).

The relation between incentive mechanisms and performance is shown in figure 7.9:

The absence of incentive mechanisms, or the presence of weak ones only, depends on the size of the organisation (no human resources management service in small organisations), on the associative culture, and on the socioprofessional profile and personality of the OSO's top volunteer administrators. It explains, and can also be explained by, a deficiency in or absence of a control culture on the part of the actors. A new incentive system for individuals, teams, and groups should be developed with close connections to the performance assessment system. The connections between the performance assessment system and the existing reporting, planning, and control systems should be carefully considered to avoid overlap and contradiction.

The Absence of Control on the Part of the Actors

The evaluation of persons working in an organisation corresponds to several objectives: to inform them about their performance, to motivate them, to establish communication between managers and employees, to facilitate the sense of responsibility, and to determine objective criteria in order to establish incentive mechanisms on the basis of professional investment by staff and their identification with the objectives to be achieved.

Evaluation, corollary to control, appears to be a taboo in the associative sector—and even more in the case of a volunteer this person is in place to do and experience something different than he or she did during his or her professional activity. He or she acts in accordance with rationales other than those of an executive in a company. The desire to control and objectively evaluate the work of the volunteer administrators can be taken negatively given the volunteer' democratic legitimacy. Unclear objectives and lack of clarity in the use of the federation's resources turn into a tendency to favour objectives in qualitative or ideological terms, which induces more difficulty regarding measurements of efforts and makes it possible to maintain a strong culture of unspoken issues and of ambiguity that is often a guarantee of political stability. If ambiguity can be favourable, notably in relations with external partners (particularly the Ministry of Youth and Sport for an NSF), it appears problematic in political systems and internally and can lead to inertia and conflicts.

The precise analysis of tasks, of the organisation of functions, and of the information circuits, as well as the study of working regulations and control mechanisms in the OSOs, generally led to the conclusion that a great degree of autonomy is left to unpaid and paid staff members.

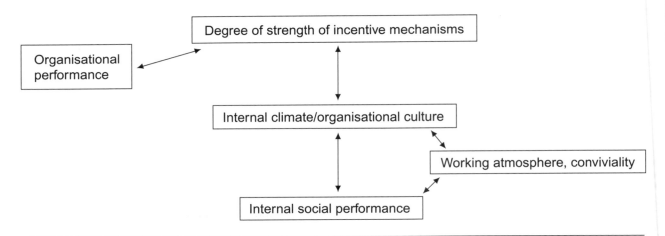

Figure 7.9 Relationship between incentive mechanisms and performance.

Formalising management systems (development plan, procedures, job descriptions) seems to have an internal structuring effect when it is not perceived by salaried staff or volunteer administrators as a burden (too many evaluation criteria) or as useless (inappropriate criteria or criteria that are not used) or as hindering the emergence of new ideas and flexibility. A convention regarding objectives between the Ministry of Sport and the federations constitutes a system that incites formalisation and makes the federation progress in its strategic approach (notably in the organisation of the high level sport system).

In fact, organisational control can operate on three levels: operational control, management control, and strategic control. The strategic cycle and the OSO's policy thus blend into each other.

The first level (operational control) controls the achievement of, and conditions for achieving the various tasks necessary in order to implement the OSO's activities. The importance of this depends on the administrative structure and the formalisation that accompanies it (procedures, reports, balance sheets, regularity, culture of the directors, etc.). The motivation of the actors and the quality of the work by salaried staff do not necessarily seem linked to their evolution within the structure and to their progression. The control system, when it exists, can thus be highly lacking as regards motivation and legitimacy in the eyes of the staff.

Table 7.3 provides a summarised view of the very different evaluation and control systems for the three categories of actors.

Management control—a tool for controlling costs—is closer to budget management that provides only a partial vision of strategic issues and very limited information on the pertinence of hypotheses that rule the choice of the major strategic directions and their respective costs for the structure. This type of budgetary control is sometimes completed by regulations regarding procedures for purchasing and financial control of the leagues by the federation. In all cases, management control and analytical accounting do not have the same meaning as they do in an entrepreneurial framework.

Strategic control consists of comparing the objectives achieved with those forecast. It still appears to be taboo in the world of the OSOs, because the strategic cycle for the development plan is based on the Olympiad (the election cycle) in most cases. Formalising systems depends on the culture of the major volunteer administrators and on the levels of structure, but also on the obligation to report to partners.

The recent approach to the development project taken by the French canoe–kayak federation appears to be new in the sport world: It is formalised, diffused, and even the subject of media

Table 7.3 **Categories of Olympic Sport Organizations' Actors and Evaluation, Control, and Incentive Mechanisms**

Category of actors/ Control and evaluation system	Volunteer administrators	Technical (sport) experts	Permanent administrative salaried staff
Criteria for evaluating work carried out	Taboo	Precise	Precise to imprecise (depending on organisational and managerial culture and tasks carried out)
Main incentive mechanism	Recognition (social)	Recognition of work carried out and status	Status; progression of salary
Evaluation criteria and incentive mechanism	Imprecise	Precise (sport result)	Imprecise and often not taken into account
Control of actors	Very low (total autonomy)	Low (high degree of autonomy)	Depending on the executives' culture (double supervision, elected officials and managerial)

focus. This shows the public the federation's desire to make its actions visible. Since 1984, the executive committee has implemented a self-evaluation approach, and the evaluation is based on the federation's development indicators and the degree to which objectives have been achieved. Its presentation seems, in our opinion, to illustrate an interesting approach for the world of federations.

From 16 general objectives and 96 sub-objectives for the 1993-1997 development plan, the French canoe–kayak federation has reduced its 1998-2002 plan to 4 main objectives and 26 sub-objectives. The method was to constitute a working group representing the various levels of the federation's system (salaried staff, volunteer administrators of the club and of the federation) in order to build up the 1998-2002 development project. This development plan, moreover, was intentionally created to overlap two electoral periods in order to avoid the involvement of electoral issues.

The stages of the development project were summarised by the formula "think it, say it, do it" (see www.ffcanoe.asso.fr).

"Thinking" corresponded to presenting the development priorities retained by the working group and then by the executive office and the federation's board. The priorities emerged following exchanges of opinion within the framework of interregional seminars or activities or multidisciplinary committees.

"Saying" meant drawing up a summary document and a balance sheet for 1993-1997 covering the various contributions from the federation's activities. A communications strategy made it possible, thanks to various documents (balance sheet, project, poster, regional projects), to pass the message on regarding the results obtained and the federation's future commitments.

"Doing" consisted of drawing up criteria for implementation tools and tools for the annual monitoring of the 1998-2002 project. The approach was, first, to create regional logs. On a national level, this took the form of providing financial resources and building up the federation's budget based on the priorities retained for the year, plus a regional and local equivalent of the federation's development project.

The problem is that extremely scrupulous control and extremely high external communication of results can be perceived as a political sanction for the team in place, meaning a double-edged sword in the associative world. Weak control in associative organisations, even large ones like the NSFs, is generally explained by the ideology and the associative culture.

That is why the new development project was based on a 10-year period, 2002 to 2012, with five main orientations and 16 priorities, four challenges per priority (one challenge each for national headquarters, regional branch, departmental branch, clubs).

The absence of control at strategic, managerial, and operational levels can generate a method of management by affection and, more globally, by subjectivity. For this reason, salaried staff close to the president must have both technical knowledge and relational and political know-how requiring a strong tolerance of ambiguity within the organisational functioning.

Use by management of affection among volunteers and salaried staff explains the fact that control and evaluation methods are highly empirical. The method of coordination by affection (pleasure people take in being together, conviviality, lack of clarity in relations of powers and prerogatives, etc.) explains the importance of informal, underground means of coordination between paid staff and volunteer administrators. For this reason, changes to premises and generally the physical organisation of the premises have a significant impact on communication between persons, which can be problematic given the impersonal and powerful means of communication in this type of organisation.

In such a context, a clear risk exists that the organisation will be perceived as a frustrating place to work for the salaried staff and in fact as a structure that blocks personal progression (one in which the work is routine, administrative, and lacking in "image," little possibility of taking responsibility, a feeling of uselessness, a lack of comprehension of the project that the person's work is involved with, relational difficulties, lack of reflection on the status of staff, supervision by volunteer administrators as a burden on salaried staff, no sanctioning of the quality of work carried out, etc.). An organisation can be considered deficient when it does not permit the competencies of the salaried staff it employs to develop. It is not an aside to note that professional mobility appears to be much higher in the entrepreneurial world than in the associative one: Opportunities for employment to move from the associative world to the professional, commercial world in fact remain fairly rare (except within event organisation or marketing).

Bathed in such a culture, the associative world of the OSOs runs the risk of being characterised by the syndrome of rendering staff irresponsible: There are no instructions from the volunteer administrators to paid staff, or the instructions are incoherent or contradictory, meaning that salaried staff cannot work effectively because of the unpaid staff and are not given a sense of responsibility.

It is, in fact, by no means simple to manage when departments are strongly decentralised, when the homogeneity of the various categories of staff is low, when the feeling of belonging to the organisation on the part of certain specialists is nonexistent, when the authority of the administrative management comes up against the counter-power of the volunteer administrators, and when official supervision increases the pressure brought to bear. However, the manager can seek to benefit from the high number of different levels and staff in the organisation by using this circumstance positively thanks to efficient integration processes that give precedence to interpersonal relationships. Informal coordination also plays a decisive role in small organisations (5 to 50 salaried employees in most OSOs) in which the average number of meetings of the OSO's management team and of the executive committee sometimes indicates

a lack of moments of concert for the executive and control bodies.

Growth in the size of the organisation justifies the need for coordination and control if this situation tends to favour and multiply opportunists who lead it astray. An increase in coordination functions that are not really productive and the absence of a culture of controlling the actors (on a level of principles and tools) can mean that the effectiveness of the structure degenerates rapidly. Delegating the operational management of dossiers in the OSOs to permanent staff (paid or unpaid) does, however, demand control of the results achieved by salaried directors in order to avoid any functional dispersion that harms coherence and the organisational function.

The relation between deficiency/lack of a control culture and actors/performance is shown in figure 7.10.

Beyond external controls, the internal control of the organisation and its actors must in theory be carried out at a triple level, which explains the extent of the agency costs linked to these control systems:

• Control by volunteer administrators over salaried directors and technical experts (and the inverse, even if the control mechanism is an unspoken one; in this case it is more appropriate to speak of influence systems than control systems). In certain OSOs, there are special procedures concerning the use of the OSO's money (expense commitment procedure, tenders for purchases of above EUR 15,000).

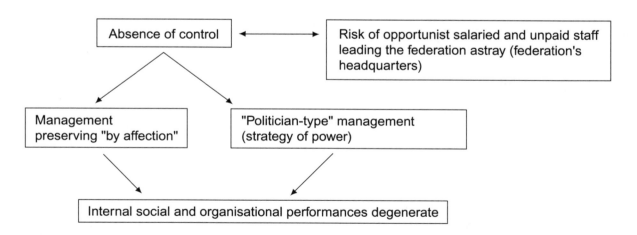

Figure 7.10 Relationship between deficient control and actor performance.

- Control by the salaried directors over coworkers (and the inverse, which can explain a method of involvement whose extent varies).

- Control by the OSO's headquarters in relation to the leagues, committees, and clubs (and inversely, the control can be similar to a political sanction of the OSO)

These controls apply to four main areas: the sport results (the training system and the elite sport section), finances (resources generated, operating costs), administration, and criteria that could be placed under the heading of development (growth in members, development of the sport). These areas of control operate at the level of the headquarters and the level of the federation's system.

Political Sclerosis

Weak control, given the democratic, associative ideal, can often be explained by the political sclerosis present in the OSO's system. The sclerosis can operate on two main levels: between the OSO's system (NSF headquarters, leagues, area committees, and clubs) and its headquarters and also between volunteer administrators from the headquarters and salaried management staff. These levels of conflict can be linked. Power struggles generate conflicts of prerogatives.

Deficiencies and dysfunction in the OSOs' electoral systems can explain the inertia and the absence of democratisation revealed in a fair number of OSOs. The volunteer administrators (elected to the voluntary board of directors) tend to defend the interest of the structure from which they come (league, NSF), sometimes even against the interests of the organisation. More globally, a dissociation of personal and general interest within the OSO's system appears to be particularly difficult to achieve.

In OSOs, strategic and organisational behaviour appear to be legitimised with respect to performance as much as by political and elective issues. At the absolute limit, the system's management can be summed up as the dominant actors' capacity for being re-elected. The perversion of the current election systems in OSOs (e.g., no limitation of the mandate of the president, indirect democracy) often makes it possible to ensure that mandates are renewed without any real democratic debate and also

makes it possible to explain, in certain cases, the discouragement of volunteers.

One of the main causes of political sclerosis (beyond personal conflicts inherent to any organisation) is the gap between the rhythm of innovation and organisation between the federation (or a NOC), its leagues, and its area committees. It could be also the case between the professional league and the federation (interest conflicts between clubs and national team). This sclerosis could generate a virtually complete rupture of communication and confidence between the federation's base and summit for political reasons.

Implementing a development project for the OSOs requires cohesion and dialogue between all structures, notably to bond them together and create coherency in the relations between clubs, area committees, and the federation's headquarters. This cohesion seems to develop based on the existing confidence among the actors in the system, which makes it possible to avoid conflicts of power and prerogatives. For this reason, the cement within the OSO's network appears to be less than for the hierarchy (agency relationship with explicit contracts) than that of confidence between the actors (convention constructions based on implicit content) between the OSO's headquarters, its system, and its relations with its environment.

Conflicts give rise to issues that are negative. Managing consists of creating a progressive spiral through the generation of collaborative types of behaviour, with the aim of making it possible for each actor to find new sources of power in order to supply new situations of negotiation. The counterparts thus transform the negotiation into a positive issue.

In the case of the OSOs, political sclerosis demonstrates that management systems do not necessarily arise as a result of desiring or seeking performance but also because of the capacity to preserve the political interests of persons in office in the federations, where the possibility for negotiation are numerous and take place depending on the interests of the actors.

The key factors of failure have been revealed (see table 7.4), but study of the relationship of balance between differentiation/integration (Lawrence and Lorsch 1973) at the origine of the OSO's performance can be envisaged only

Table 7.4 **Key Failure Factors**

Deficient information and reporting systems	Complexity of incentive mechanisms	Weak control over the actors	Political sclerosis
Solutions			
Introduce strategic, managerial, and operational reporting systems; share the cost of information with stakeholders that have interest in the organisation	Global/individual, financial/nonfinancial (for volunteers and paid staff) linked to the strategic plan	Human resources tools: procedures, job description, staff training, annual evaluation meeting, for example	Reduce gap of innovation between OSO headquarters and OSO system; avoid dysfunction in electoral system

in a dialectic perspective, taking into account not only all the integrating factors but also the dynamics and interaction of internal and external changes that the organisation undergoes.

7.3 Necessary Changes and Adaptations

In a federalist structure (NOCs, NSFs, and IFs), managing performance must take place on a double level: in the OSO's system and its headquarters. This interlinking aspect common to all pyramid-type organisations explains all the complexity of managing this type of organisation in order to integrate the opportunities and threats from the socioeconomic environment. The degree of openness of the OSO's headquarters and system regarding its environment will in fact determine the degree of instability of the balance between differentiation and integration (Lawrence and Lorsch 1973).

Differentiation concerns "the differences of orientation on the part of the functional major volunteer administrators, the different ways in which administrators project their actions over time within the various bodies of the organisation (short or long term), the various types of behaviour of the volunteer administrators toward their colleagues or department (interpersonal orientation), the differentiation between the functional units (formal structure)" (Lawrence and Lorsch 1973).

Integration is the "duality of collaboration that exists among departments that must unite their efforts in order to satisfy the demands of the environment and the organisational strategies to achieve this goal" (Lawrence and Lorsch 1973).

This degree of openness can be explained by the fact that some OSOs adopt a strategic analysis in market terms (global reflection about strategy in order to benefit from all the information from the environment); others conduct analysis in product terms (internal reflection on the federation's various products and services to be offered to licensed athletes and those practising the sport); still others remain hidebound, using a purely Coubertinian analysis (which one can define as attracting a minimum of members to supply the creation of an elite).

In the first case, the system is completely open to the environment; but it is less so in the second. In the third, it is closed, and its permeability to external signals is low. It is clear that the organisation's potential for performance, notably economic and financial, will vary according to its degree of openness to external elements. The greater the openness, the greater the performance potential will be, but also the more vulnerable the position of the organisation regarding competition and the pressures it may encounter within the conditions for its development. The more open-minded the OSO, the stronger the differentiation between its headquarters and its system must be, and consequently, the more powerful and multiple the integrating mechanisms must be to maintain or improve the organisation's performance.

The theory of Lawrence and Lorsch (1973) is that in order to maintain a good level of performance in an organisation, a balance between differentiation and integration is necessary; the higher the differentiation within the organisation, the stronger and more powerful the integrating mechanisms must be. The balance between differentiation and integration, the performance potential, and the level of each

OSO's performance profile will vary depending on the organisation's degree of openness to its environment.

Raising questions on the state of balance between differentiation and integration in fact invites reflection on the conditions for organisational change and the dialectic necessary between the differentiation–integration coupling that the organisation's directors must succeed in mastering. We present the two key points that appear to explain strategic and organisational change in the OSOs. When a major change takes place, there is a risk of rupture in the balance between differentiation and integration. Insufficient strategic repositioning and the resulting adjustment of integrating mechanisms may lead to a rupture in the balance between differentiation and integration and thus the emergence of dysfunction and crises that could result in a drop in certain performances and more generally in the organisation's performance potential. For this reason, the question of strategic and organisational change and the possible rupture of the differentiation–integration balance implies research on methods of reconstruction around the three key variables: the organisation's strategy, structure, and culture.

The Two Key Points Regarding Strategic and Organisational Change

Studying the balance between differentiation and integration naturally leads to an interest in organisational change. All organisations must, at various points in their life, face change. In OSOs, this mostly relates to what is described by Pettigrew (1990) as "a somewhat political process of decisions and negotiations." This author does not have a vision of change in which the executives decide and the others apply. Change revolves around three interlinked elements: "the context (internal and external), the process itself and the content of the change (technology, markets, culture, etc.)."

In the light of OSOs case studies, two major points appear to explain an evolving or revolutionary type of change in the OSOs. These two fundamental factors are close to those revealed by Romanelli and Tushman (1994): the major changes within the environment, which theo-retically demand a modification of strategy, and the succession of executives, notably a charismatic executive, since this can condition a change of strategy, of internal functioning, and the global stability of the system.

In the first case and for an NSF, it is not really the position of the Ministry of Sport that appears decisive, but rather that of an essential private partner: a television channel, a patron, a sponsor, or the like. This situation generally concerns a private partner that provides a significant financial income for the OSO (20% or more of the federation's budget) or is the first major private partner (or both) and the possible precursor of other partners. The arrival or withdrawal of this partner is a vector for multiple changes in the national federation and for an approach aimed at satisfying this partner with a view to the partner's remaining loyal, to attracting other partners, and to manage dependence.

In the second case, the role of an integrator-type leader appears to be fundamental to maintaining the major areas of balance revealed. A change of president in an OSO constitutes a key moment of transition that it is essential to manage, notably for presidents who have been present within the structure for a long time and who can embody the federation. Whether a visionary or a negotiator, the leader is the person who lends legitimacy to a strategy and creates a social architecture, or determines a challenge, or does both. Based on his or her capacity to assimilate the need for change and his or her legitimacy following election, this person may embody a vision or a new modernity, or represent the stability that guarantees maintenance of the balance of power and the interests of the dominant actors (volunteer administrators of powerful leagues, national technical directors, salaried general directors).

The legitimacy of the volunteer administrators comes not only from their hierarchical position but also from their ability to understand the culture of their organisation and develop their dream of its future. This takes the form of the capacity to provide a vision of the conditions for the development of the sport, fixing the quantitative elements for future growth ("to have X licensed athletes, X number of competitors, X medals, X sport results," etc.), which, at a given moment, constitute an objective that is impossible to achieve but is nevertheless achieved or exceeded (see utopian projects by judo and tennis in the 1970s that were nevertheless achieved).

This ideological phase, when it coincides with a favourable environment, explains the remarkable success of certain federations (international volleyball federation, 1990-2000; French tennis federation between 1975 and 1985; French hiking federation from 1992 to 2000)—one more continuous and regular than others (judo)—that spreads to the aura and legitimacy of their presidents.

The politicisation of internal relations seems to develop either during brutal changes imposed by the environment or through a modification in the balance of internal power relations (the extent of manoeuvring allowed by the structure explains the development of opportunist behaviour by the actors and the growth in informal differentiation). Structure, culture, and strategy are no longer neutral issues here but can be used by the executives in power struggles aimed at protecting or destroying the interests of the dominant actors, who correspond to the key actors in the change. Depending on the situation the executive can be innovative or conservative, although the success of the change process supposes the existence of a visionary, accepted leader. Volunteers can also constitute a force within change by forming coalitions. This political type of analysis makes it possible to understand how blocking and changing forces are formed (bureaucrats, experts, culture, etc.) and how this can be circumvented. "The convergence of strategic actions is never perfect or definitive because depending on the moment, the actors who support opposed objectives can be dominant because their coalition has won or is dominant" (Mintzberg 1990, p. 223). The strategic and organisational balance thus always remains and is the objective to achieve.

Many NSFs in Europe, highly dependent on financing by their Ministry of Sport, are subject to the goodwill of their official supervisory authority for the allocation of resources. This situation renders the management situation even more complex, since the decision by one party regarding the allocation of funds to the federations is taken outside the organisation. In this context, the internal actors are little inclined to drive changes and can opt for strate-gic behaviour that is by no means offensive. Any strategic decision implies that it is possible to reply to two questions: Can one determine what it is necessary to want? And above all, is there an actor with the power to change anything?

The person initiating the change is, in almost all cases, the OSO's president, who initially, in order to anchor his or her political legitimacy, must form a coalition with other actors and can then impose change based on the credit he or she has obtained from various sources (competence, charisma, political skills, etc.). For this reason, the change process can be slow at the outset and grow as the president's legitimacy becomes stronger.

The two main change factors observed that can considerably modify the balance between differentiation and integration are both vectors of opportunities but also of risks of dysfunction or even crisis.

Rupture of Balance and the Risks of Crisis

Rupture of the balance between differentiation and integration generally takes the form of the emergence of dysfunctions and adaptation or inertia crises, whether at a headquarters level or within the OSO's system. Sooner or later, this rupture has an impact on the organisation's global performance and its performance potential.

In an association, the causes of dysfunction or crisis are usually less financial than is the case in companies. For this reason, crisis in an association can take on more varied forms. Dysfunction that can lead to a crisis can have the following origins:

• External: This type of imbalance arises from the lethargy of markets or relations with the supervisory authority. Possible causes are a drop in the number of licensed athletes, a drop in performance by the elite, poor progression in the number of licensed athletes when the number of those practising the sport is on the increase, and conflicts between federation, league, and committee.

• Internal: Possible causes are shortcomings in the decision-taking system (no decisions taken by volunteer administrators or decisions not taken rapidly enough to react to market requirements), weak technical and organisational function, unsatisfactory differentiation, sclerosis of the system because of the political organisation, excessive focus on one dimension of performance to the detriment of others, change in the president corresponding to a radical change in method of functioning.

Pujol (1995) proposes four major types of dysfunction within sport organizations to explain the phenomenon of crisis in associations.

- The first is an ongoing drop in the motivation of the volunteer administrators. This form of crisis appears more problematic for small associations than for large associations such as the sport organisations, since the image-enhancing position of the administrator is rarely abandoned in the large OSOs. It is therefore a more latent crisis of noninvestment on the part of the volunteer administrators and the abandonment of power (leadership, initiatives, etc.) or conservation of power for reasons of personal interest.

- The second is an increase in tension between volunteer administrators and salaried staff.

- The third is a financial type of dysfunction (in the case of the OSOs this can be insufficient resources, bad management of expenses, or embezzlement of funds).

- The fourth is a heavy organisational structure (this heaviness can affect the efficiency and effectiveness of the organisation and its capacity to implement actions). We can add a fifth type of dysfunction that may characterise a pyramid-type organisation such as an IF or an NSF, which is a gap of reactivity and structuring between the summit (the headquarters) and the entities that apply, or control the application of, the federation's policy (leagues, area committees, and clubs).

According to Pujol (1995, p. 310), "Before the association reaches a critical phase, the major types of dysfunction were probably not as numerous or did not yet deserve the term 'major'." The crisis is often formed as a result of a cumulative process whereby a number of actual causes mean that the threshold of certainty for the association is overstepped.

When the crisis has actually arisen, all the major areas of dysfunction do not act equally.

Their ranking, depending on their contribution to the critical situation, may also evolve. It may, for example, happen that two out of four of them are predominant or, alternatively, a single one predominates. The two or three other major types of dysfunction that are less active nevertheless contribute toward worsening the crisis.

There may be multiple triggers of the crisis. It can be internal even if it arose externally. It can be external and not integrated internally.

Pujol identifies seven situations of crisis in associations, of which five—and mainly the last two—may concern OSOs (since the first three concern, in our opinion, small associations): the crisis of initial organisation, the crisis of setting up, the crisis of confidence, the crisis of internal organisation, the diffusion crisis, the institutional crisis, and sclerosis.

The crisis of internal organisation stems from the fact that the association must face new challenges that occur because of increasing complexity and must organise itself better to harmonise the internal ambition–functioning relation; this is the main risk of crisis with respect to the federations during a period of development and strategic innovation. The diffusion crisis is revealed by the need for a good central organisation, as well as the need to be demanding and rigorous and the need for adequate control; this is the main risk of crisis incurred by federations during a period of maturity in their development. The association becomes an institution with a hierarchical structure in which the internal and external power ratios are particularly present. It gives the impression of being a heavy, impersonal structure in which the members may feel they are kept at a distance. This is the reign of rules, programmes, and bureaucratic procedures aimed at normalising behaviour. All this means an atmosphere that favours tension, notably between unpaid and salaried staff. This is the main risk of crisis for federations whose coordination is necessarily complex given the size of the structure. Sclerosis occurs when the association's objective is no longer to serve its vocation but rather, even if this is unspoken, to continue to exist in order to serve other purposes (personal objectives on the part of unpaid and salaried executives) while taking advantage of public money; in this latter case, there is thus a clear inversion of objectives.

The relationship between performance and the rupture of balance between differentiation and integration is shown in figure 7.11.

The possible emergence of dysfunctions or crises, in a more normative perspective, invites reflection on the adjustments necessary, notably in the case of major internal or external changes, given the integrating mechanisms that the volunteer administrators and paid managers have at their disposal.

Necessary Adjustments Surrounding Strategy, Structure, and Culture

We have shown that the more dynamic and complex the environments were, the stronger the OSOs' organisational chart should have been. In parallel, the stronger the organisation's differentiation, the more extensive the integration and coordination mechanisms must be, or the organisation must carry out a "retro-differentiation" (Koenig 1996). If the environment is heterogeneous, seeking to reduce the organisation's internal diversity is not the solution; rather the organisation needs to balance this by integrating an equivalent force.

The first method of integration on the level of the federation's headquarters is the hierarchical authority (creation of new hierarchies). This form of integration is often sufficient when the organisation's structural differentiation is weak, but generally proves insufficient after a time. Formal structures such as procedures, planning, evaluation, and control systems may then strengthen integration. However, when the organisation's differentiation is significant, hierarchical authority by a single person becomes insufficient and the formal systems become inoperative. In this case, several coordination mechanisms are available to managers, such as work by liaison and coordination persons or integration groups (director general, liaison committees, working groups, more autonomous management of the departments, etc.). The problem can come from a politicisation of the function of these people. Certain OSOs also set up a dual system of functioning, that is, an volunteer administrator/ salaried director to ensure the coordination of major projects.

In all cases, however, the director general or director of administration usually plays an essential role of coordination via the counter-power and the force of the proposals that he or she offers to the volunteer administrators. This counter-power of the general director (if this function exists) will be all the stronger thanks to his or her legitimacy or even charisma, coming from multiple sources: technical competencies, his or her history in sport, the work he or she has achieved, how long he or she has served the OSO, and so on will be important and will

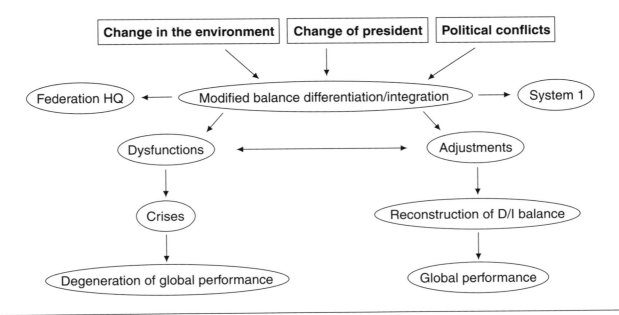

Figure 7.11 Relationship between performance and unbalanced internal organisation.

be acknowledged by the volunteer administrators. For this reason, certain OSOs take extreme care when recruiting this person (see the case of some federations, in which the technical and general directors often come from within the federation and are often former champions). On the other hand, this is also why volunteer administrators do not wish to recruit or install a strong personality in such a function. Not doing so makes it easier for them to control the power.

In order to guarantee the balance between differentiation and integration, work on strategic analysis emphasises the necessary adaptability of the structure and of the strategy. The general idea of strategists is as follows: In order to avoid becoming hidebound in routines and programmes that condemn its activity to a static, immobile perception, the organisation must develop the structural means to fight inertia. To do so, the organisation combats excessive consensus and tolerates a reasonable degree of opposition, avoids an excess of harmony, and favours minor, progressive adjustments. This is the principle of self-organisation. This, however, has dangers: It supposes that the members of the organisation tolerate ambiguity and have a low resistance to change. The critical task here will be a sound evaluation of the level of differentiation. Executives who are above all interested in conserving the stability of their organisation can opt for a strategy of reducing the necessity for differentiation.

In fact, the OSOs can be presented as non-homogeneous systems within which rationality and irrationality, harmony and conflict, order and disorder, coexist and interact. The role of the managers (volunteer or paid) consists of managing these dualities. For example, the presence of too many volunteers in the decision-making process can lead to low reactivity and slowness in the decision-taking process and the application of the decisions by salaried staff; or inversely, a preponderance of salaried staff in the decision-making process can degenerate the organisational culture and collaboration between unpaid and paid staff. For this reason, one must acknowledge that

combinations of human, technical, financial, and organisational factors exist that are effective within a given context and period and not in others. These combinations are multiple and change over time and over the life of an organisation. There is indeed a permanent reconstruction of the balance between differentiation and integration, whether by means of adjustments (integrating mechanisms) or major changes in the three reference elements defined (system of governance, federation's network, size and positioning of the OSO in the channel). These latter, in order to be effective, must preserve the alignment of the strategy/structure/culture triptych, which appears fundamental.

The entire problem, for the manager, is to manage the fact that these elements do not change at the same speed: Culture demands time and strong mechanisms in order to change, while strategy can be defined and implemented relatively rapidly.

When one of these two major changes that we have observed breaks the relationship between culture, strategy, and structure, a risk of deterioration or of breaking up the differentiation–integration balance occurs. In order to preserve this balance, managers can slow down the implementation of the strategy, seeking to preserve the culture and to find compromise on the level of structure, notably in relations and prerogatives between paid staff and volunteer administrators.

The entrance via which the change takes place and the integrating mechanisms are forged is also decisive for permitting a balance between differentiation and integration. Here (see figure 7.12), we find the "three paths likely to drive change" proposed by Bréchet (1997, p. 24), that is, the formal structures instituted and the cultures and interaction between the actors.

These three entrances provide an excellent position for volunteer administrators when seeking a balance between differentiation and integration.

Figure 7.13 shows the relationship between strategy, structure, culture, and performance from which the control of the balance between differentiation and integration originates.

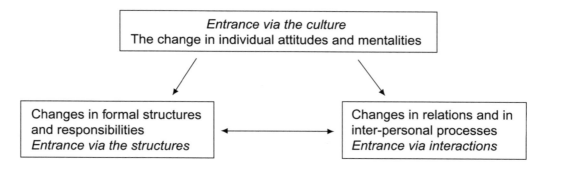

Figure 7.12 Bréchet's three paths to drive change.

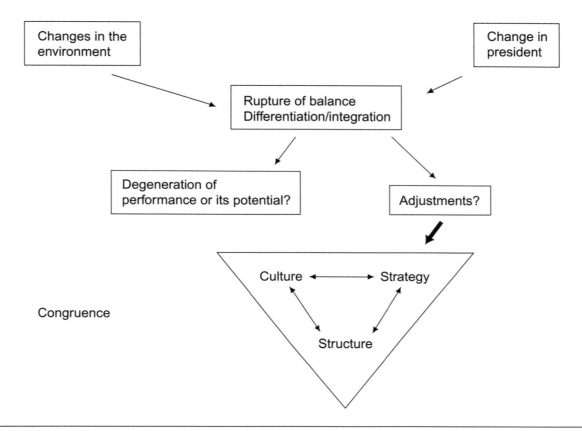

Figure 7.13 The balance between differentiation and integration.

Conclusion

Today foreseeing the future of OSOs is similar to raising questions about the durability of their status and, above all, of their legitimacy given their current functioning methods.: The effectiveness, efficiency, and transparency of the management of OSOs are becoming the crucial aspects examined by the members and by the public and private partners. Insofar as the organisations become more complex and the organizational tasks more numerous and differentiated (as has been the case for most OSOs during the last 10 years), the need for more precise measurement tools becomes greater. At the same time, the difficulties involved in the process of performance evaluation increase along with the growth of the organization, and the traditional criteria of evaluation founded almost exclusively on medal counts and number of affiliated members become insufficient since they represent measures only of the final output, without providing any hints about lower-level objectives or other key factors of the final performance. The OSO performance evaluation methods that we have presented in this book require a stronger political commitment and a further improvement of the OSOs' internal communication systems, since the different components of an OSO (including the decentralized structures and the clubs) must be informed and aware not only of the priorities, but also of the nature and scope of their assessment process (see Esposito and Madella 2003).

For steering the performance of OSOs, we have proposed a specific framework developed as a result of case studies of OSOs and theoretical management research in the field. Three essential elements constitute the strategic performance mix of an OSO: the form and functioning conditions of the OSO's governance, the quality of its network, and the size of the economic channel for its sport and the position of the OSO within this channel. Concerning the first principle, new mechanisms for governing an OSO were proposed. Multiple-convention strategies can significantly favour the achievement of the two last principles of functioning.

These generic principles constitute the strategic framework of the OSOs, but other internal integration mechanisms for the adjustment of internal functioning principles are also important for steering the operational performance mix of the OSOs. Professionalization under the control of unpaid executives, the organisational culture as an essential participative mechanism, and partnership and services to stakeholders represent key factors of success in handling the complexity of managing a system and a network of organisations. In fact, the future of the OSOs seems to demand a major evolution of principles and management methods in order to guarantee these organizations the reactivity necessary to respond to the rapidity and complexity of the evolution of their environment.

Epilogue

The management of Olympic sport organisa-tions (OSOs) is entering a new era. Until the beginning of the 1980s, the OSO system was one of simple administration. After a period of development, notably commercial, of their activities in the 1990s, OSOs are now embark-ing on a period of strategic and performance management. The growing formalisation of their strategy requires reflection regarding their values and identity. The strategic project is a legitimising tool that also reveals the new directions for driving performance: it enables priority action-areas to be identified, objectives to be formalised, and actions to be structured as performance indicators.

Driving performance makes it possible to enter into a rationalisation project within which we have attempted to identify the key success factors for these highly political organisations. These organisations must exist as a democracy in which volunteers and salaried staff can work together on a common project, while indicating the direction to follow without any easily iden-tifiable or measurable performance criteria.

The importance of the issues at stake related to the sport and Olympic phenomenon and the growth in size (budget, number of salaried staff, members, partners, etc.) of the organisations behind it today imply new challenges to driving performance and strategic leadership in terms of adaptation and capacity to react.

The first challenge comes from the disintegra-tion of these organisations' traditional frontiers, which requires setting up extremely powerful managerial integration mechanisms. This disin-tegration can be explained by the development of partnerships of all kinds, but is also related to another notion: the emergence of groups of organisations. The federative structures such as the IOC, the NOCs, and the IFs and NSFs cre-ated a number of affiliates for legal, financial or fiscal reasons, or for the sake of transparency. These groups offer development potential of a kind that is at times new. However, they also render the management of the OSOs and their relations with their "subsidiaries" even more complex.

The second challenge is to lend meaning to their strategic project and to the players who steer it and take part in it. Commercial develop-ment related to sports events and sport-for-all philosphy raises the question of the traditional organisations' capacity to harvest the fruit of their efforts and to justify the reason behind the project in question, which is above all and by nature a humanist one (education, health, integration, peace, etc.). The question of soli-darity within each international federation, and more widely within the sport and Olym-pic movement, is central in order to define the major redistributors and the way in which this redistribution is implemented.

The third challenge is to introduce new management methods during a period when the world of non-governmental organisations appears as a new recourse. This development has occurred as a result of the failure of the market and public authorities to develop the dimension of sport and to regulate a certain number of problems related to sport (doping, violence, corruption, harm to the environment, etc.).

We hope that this book will help you as you accept these three challenges and contribute toward better management of OSOs.

Emmanuel Bayle and Jean-Loup Chappelet
July 2004

Appendix A

Sample Strategic Plans of Canadian Sport Organisations

Canadian Olympic Committee: www.olympic.ca/EN/organization/publications/strategicplan.shtml

Diving Canada Plongeon: www.diving.ca/new_layout/index_e.html

Tennis Canada: www.tenniscanada.com/federation/english (click on "Inside TC" link)

Canadian Yachting Association: www.sailing.ca/about/strategic.shtm

Canadian Cycling Association: www.canadian-cycling.com/e2/about/index.htm

Field Hockey Canada: www.fieldhockey.ca/e/administration/governance/strategic_frame.htm

Appendix B

U.S. National Governing Bodies' Visions and/or Mission Statements

National governing body	Date	Vision and/or mission
Archery	2001	To develop and promote all aspects of archery with the ultimate goal of producing Olympic and World Champions.
Badminton	2002	USA Badminton will foster the growth of badminton in the United States of America and competitive excellence by U.S. athletes in international and Olympic competition.
Baseball	2001	USA Baseball is the sole organization responsible for selecting, training, and supporting the USA Baseball Olympic Team, the USA Baseball National Team, the USA Baseball Junior National Team (18-under), and the USA Baseball Youth National Team (16-under) which participate in international competitions each year. USA Baseball is responsible for promoting and developing the game of baseball on the grassroots level, both nationally and internationally. As the commissioner's office for amateur baseball, USA Baseball is a resource center for it's various membership groups, fans, and players.
Basketball	2000	Develop, select and support USA Basketball's teams for men and women, in the very best manner possible, in order that these teams achieve at the highest level of excellence in national and international competition with the ultimate expectation of consistently winning gold medals in World Championship and Olympic Competitions.
Biathlon	09/14/99	• To prepare United States athletes to achieve their best possible results in international competition, demonstrating steady improvement with consistent top 10 finishes in World Cup competition and medal winning performances in Olympic Games. • To Promote an awareness of, participation in and support of the sport of biathlon to the broadest possible audience nationwide, which will develop and maintain an athlete feeder system, increase membership and volunteers, and improve our marketability, which will all support our competitive mission.
Bobsled	1999	To establish and maintain global preeminence in all aspects of bobsled competition, as defined by sustained Olympic and other elite international medal results by multiple competitors. The Federation desires to foster the broadest possible participation in the sports of bobsled and skeleton, to facilitate the improvement and enjoyable participation of all member athletes, and to promote the universal ideals of the Olympic Games.
Bowling	January 2002	USA Bowling selects, trains, and supports TEAM USA and provides coaching programs.

We are indebted to Bob Gambardella for providing us with this data.

(continued)

National governing body	Date	Mission
Boxing	07/11/02	To establish the United States as a dominant force in international competitions.
Canoe–kayak	02/11/00	Build and sustain competitive excellence in the sport of canoe and kayak racing.
Curling	11/7/99	The USCA represents, governs, and promotes the sport nationally. The USCA is committed to providing leadership, education, and innovative programs to facilitate growth, public awareness, access, and competitive opportunities. The USCA is dedicated to the enhancement of personal development and enjoyment as well as competitive excellence for curlers at all levels.
Cycling	1999	Sustained international competitive success through the continued development of competition cycling in the United States.
Diving	2000	U.S. Diving is a national sports organization dedicated to the pursuit of excellence in the Olympic and World diving arena.
Equestrian	2001	The mission of the United States Equestrian Team is to develop, train, select, and fund horse/rider combinations capable of competitive excellence that will successfully represent the United States in international equestrian competitions in the three Olympic disciplines of Dressage, Eventing, and Show Jumping, as well as in the non-Olympic disciplines of Endurance, Driving, and Vaulting.
Fencing	January 2000	The mission of the USFA is to provide programs, services, and opportunities that will enable athletes from novice to Olympian to reach their maximum potential. To promote the sport of fencing in the United States.
Field hockey	01/01/00	The mission of the USFHA is to foster and develop the sport providing participation and development opportunities for players, coaches, officials, and administrators; to set a consistent standard of excellence in playing, coaching officiating and administration both domestically and internationally at all levels; to select and prepare teams to participate successfully in the Olympic Games, Pan American Games and other domestic and international competitions and to represent the United States and the sport by serving as ambassadors of good will while promoting a positive organizational image.
Figure skating	1999	The mission of the United States Figure Skating Association is to provide programs to encourage participation and achievement in the sport of figure skating on ice.
Gymnastics	1999	To encourage participation and the pursuit of excellence in all aspects of gymnastics.
Ice hockey	2002	To promote the growth of hockey in America and provide the best possible experience for all participants by encouraging, developing, advancing, and administering the sport of Ice Hockey.
Karate	2001	• To offer financial incentives to developmental instructors/coaches in order to compel those who are most successful in developing elite athletes to share their technical acumen within their peer group of elite teachers. • To make the highest levels of technical instruction readily and directly available to geographically remote athletes who have challenges and restrictions regarding access to the elite refinement necessary to international success. • To bring together representatives of technical Karate at every level at educational forums designed to practically address performance analysis of a group of pre-selected athletes who are deemed likely medal candidates. • Development of a common code of performance analysis is the thrust of these practical "round table."

National governing body	Date	Mission
Judo	2001	Win medals at every single level of international competition in which we participate in a manner commensurate with being a model representative of the United States.
Luge	1999	It is our mission, in the spirit of the Olympic Movement, to provide for the achievement of excellence in the sport of luge, with the highest degree of sportsmanship and victory as the standards. We shall recruit, develop, train and support dedicated athletes so they may represent themselves and the United States of America, with honor, in all luge competitions.
Modern pentathlon	2001	Recruit, train, and support pentathletes to win medals at Olympic, Pan American and World Championships competitions on a consistent basis and to promote the sport of pentathlon nationally and internationally
Racquetball	2000	The USRA is a non-profit corporation designed to foster and promote the development of the sports of recreational and competitive racquetball in the United States.
Roller sports	2002	USARS was incorporated for the purpose of fostering national and international amateur roller skating sports competitions on behalf of residents and citizens of the United States of America. USARS endeavors to secure for its members all the sporting benefits of organized roller sports in all its disciplines and branches; it seeks to advance the training and skills of amateur competitors, coaches, managers, and officials in the sport of roller sports regardless of race, color, religion, age, sex, or national origin; USARS exercises jurisdiction over matters pertaining to the participation of the United States amateur roller skaters in international competition; works zealously to maintain participant status in each Pan American Games and cooperates with its International Federation to secure similar status for roller sports in the Olympic Games, for which it is one of the candidate sports recognized by the IOC. USARS encourages the highest ideals of amateur sportsmanship and drug-free competitions, cooperating with such other national and international organizations as may or will foster this mission. It conscientiously performs the duties and exercises the authority of a National Governing Body as set forth in the Amateur Sports Act of 1978 and in the Constitution and by-laws of the United States Olympic Committee.
Rowing	1999	US Rowing exists to serve its members, providing leadership, and opportunities for all people to experience rowing from recreation to Olympic victory.
Sailing	2001	To encourage participation and promote excellence in sailing and racing in the United States.
Shooting	2000	• Prepare athletes to win Olympic medals • Promote the shooting sports • Govern the conduct of international shooting in the U.S.
Skiing	05/01/00	• Vision—The vision of the USSA is to make the United States of America the best in the world in Olympic skiing and snowboarding. • Mission statement—The mission of the USSA is to make the vision a reality by fielding and maintaining teams of world-class ski and snowboard athletes.
Soccer	1999	• Vision—That by the year 2005, soccer, in all its forms in the United States, should become a preeminent sport, recognized for excellence in participation, spectator appeal, international competition and gender equity. In conjunction with this, we must be in a position to compete to win the Men's World Cup by 2010 and continue to ensure that our women's team has the capacity and resources to become the number one ranking in the world. • Mission—The Mission Statement of the U.S. Soccer which supports this vision is that the United States Soccer Federation should exist to serve as the national governing body for the administration, promotion and expansion of the sport for the entire soccer community.

(continued)

National governing body	Date	Mission
Softball	01/31/02	Direct and develop the sport of softball in the United States to ensure continuing educational excellence, maximum participation, and optimum performance at all levels.
Speed skating	1999	To win Olympic and World Championship Medals.
Squash	1999	• To govern and promote the game of squash in all its forms • To promote participation in the game by the full spectrum of players and abilities, from novice to professional • To aid its members and member associations in the development, promotion, and administration of squash • To continually improve the game, the rules, and the quality of participation by all involved • To maintain a genuine spirit of true fair play and sportsmanship among all who play
Swimming	09/01/00	• USA Swimming is the National Governing Body for the sport of swimming. We administer competitive swimming in accordance with the Ted Stevens Olympic and Amateur Sports Act. We provide programs and services for our members, supporters, affiliates, and the interested public. We value these members of the swimming community, and the staff and volunteers who serve them. We are committed to excellence and the improvement of our sport. • USA Swimming strives to be the flagship National Governing Body within the U.S. Olympic Committee's family of sports organizations. • USA Swimming strives to be the number one swimming federation in the world, both in terms of competitive performance and in the overall quality of our programs and services to our members.
Synchronized swimming	2000	U.S. Synchronized Swimming exists • to provide leadership and resources for the promotion and growth of synchronized swimming • to achieve competitive excellence at all levels, and • to develop broad-based participation Paraphrased: To establish and maintain competitive excellence of our National and Olympic competitors and coaches, supported by leadership, resources, and broad base participation needed to sustain it at all levels.
Table tennis	02/22/00	USA Table Tennis is committed to providing the technical support and financial resources needed to attain World and Olympic medals for American Athletes. The organization provides programs, competition opportunities, member services, and communication outreach to encourage junior development and increased awareness of our sport nationwide.
Taekwondo	2001	To foster excellence in Taekwondo in the United States, encourage participation in all aspects of Taekwondo and to win Gold Medals in the Olympic Games.
Team handball	11/18/01	• To prepare American teams to win medals in international competitions • Develop interest and participation throughout the United States
Tennis	12/01/00	To promote and develop the growth of tennis.
Triathlon	2001	• Vision—To be the "Gold Standard" for triathlon worldwide especially on an Olympic level. USAT will seek to inspire fitness as a healthy lifestyle, create a culture for excellence in leadership and competition, and become a world leader in the sport of triathlon. • Mission—Is to make the vision a reality by providing leadership and structure for the growth and development of excellence in triathlon.

National governing body	Date	Mission
Volleyball	04/09/02	• USA Volleyball is Committed to Sustained Excellence and Exists to Lead the Sport and Promote its Unique Values. • USA Volleyball is Committed to Sustained Excellence = To consistently be the best on the court, in all our programming and in all aspects of performing our business. • Exists to Lead the Sport = To establish ourselves as the authority on volleyball in the United States and influence, through our excellence, the rest of the world. • Promote its Unique Values = To share the values of teamwork, respect for others, hard work, having fun, and playing by the rules, such that these traits are transferred into all aspects of life.
Water polo	02/09/02	• Develop and Promote the Sport and Increase Participation • Train Players, Coaches, Referees, and Volunteers • Conduct National Championships • Select, Train, and Finance USA National and Olympic Teams
Water skiing	2001	To advance and service the sport of water skiing through education, widespread participation, promotion, and sustained excellence in competition.
Weight-lifting	2001	The mission for USA Weightlifting is for our athletes to win Gold Medals in the Olympics, Pan American Games, and World Championships through the development of weightlifting in the United States of America.
Wrestling	10/01/99	As the National Governing Body, USA Wrestling shall responsibly advocate, promote, coordinate, and provide opportunities for amateur wrestlers to achieve their full human potential.

Appendix C

An Overview of Key Figures of Some Olympic Sport Organisations

Table C.1   **Key Figures for Some French Olympic and Non-Olympic National Sport Federations**

French sport federations	Number of licensed athletes in 1988	Number of licensed athletes in 1997	Number of licensed athletes in 2002	Evolution between 1988 and 2002	Total financial results 1989 (MF)	Total financial results 1997	Total financial results 2002 (MF)	Evolution between 1988 and 2002[1]	Ratio financial dependence on the Sport Ministry/budget in 1989	Ratio financial dependence in 1997	Ratio financial dependence in 2002
Athletics	120,723	152,769	165,890	+37.5%	36.8	80	92	+148%	49%	33%	36%
Rowing	31,669	52,972	64,814	+106%	13.6	24.2	32.5	+128%	63%	62%	50%
Canoeing	78,464	86,682	99,970	+21%	16.5	27	43	+160%	61%	55%	42%
Cycling	82,052	99,361	98,340	–19%	31.4	72	79	+155%	23%	19%	22%
Fencing	33,241	102,693	116,380	+221%	17.3	26	29	+70%	60%	59%	56.5%
Football	1,769,179	2,002,684	2,065,902	+17%	244.4	395	761	+212%	11%	6%	3%
Gymnastics	130,516	182,365	226,861	+74%	16.6	50	61.3	+259%	60%	27%	33.5%
Handball	178,846	221,881	318,780	+79%	32	45.5	60	+87.5%	28%	31%	30%
Swimming	128,614	173,486	216,040	+69%	41.1	39.5	51.5	+24%	33%	45%	39
Skiing	921,191	268,403	152,424	–83%	64	87	67.3	+5%	24%	27%	33
Tennis	1,364,902	1,062,786	1,067,770	–26%	240	613	806	+236%	2%	1%	0.8%
Table tennis	121,314	160,805	186,010	+54%	30	26	28	–6%	18%	33%	34.5%
Triathlon	7,084	16,178	18,590	+157%	N/A	16	20	+5%	N/A	13%	18%
Motor racing	23,816	25,256	69,200	+200%	24.6	51	76	+204%	7%	13%	10%
Orienteering	2,232	3,616	5,608	+154%	3.7	5.2	7	+90%	43%	42%	35.5%
Water skiing	11,063	11,849	14,440	+28%	6.5	9.6	10.5	+61.5%	47%	52%	50%
Squash	23,037	13,715	23,950	+4%	3.5	5.5	5.2	+43%	26%	33%	43%
Rugby League	30,065	26,393	26,004	–13%	8.5	11	13	+53%	21%	21%	23%
Rugby Union	223,726	273,459	253,152	13%	43.5	256	375	+762%	8%	2%	2.10

[1]State funding was globally stable between 1989 and 2002; this is why the evolution of total financial results comes mostly from commercial activities (sponsorship, TV rights, etc.).
N/A = non available. MF = million of French francs.
Adapted from Sports and Youth ministry and Bayle 1999.

Table C.2 Key Figures of Some U.S. Olympic and Non-Olympic National Sport Federations

U.S. sport national federations	Staff size (headquarters)[1]	Membership[2]	2003 and 2004 budget[3]
Archery	7-10 staff	6,500	$550,000 to $1,600,000
Badminton	1-6 staff	4,000	$550,000 to $1,600,000
Baseball	10 staff	N/A	$1,700,000 to $2,900,000
Basketball	10 staff	N/A	$4,100,000 to $7,500,000
Biathlon	4 staff	950	$550,000 to $1,600,000
Bobsled/skeleton	17 (8 staff + 9 coaches)	300	$3,000,000 to $4,000,000
Boxing	11 staff	30,396	$3,000,000 to $4,000,000
Canoe–kayak	8 staff	2,000	$550,000 to $1,600,000
Curling	6 staff	12,500	$550,000 to $1,600,000
Cycling	40 staff	59,000	$7,600,000 to $35,000,00
Diving	8 staff	12,000	$7,600,000 to $35,000,00
Equestrian	24 staff	82,706	$4,100,000 to $7,500,000
Fencing	15 staff	21,150	$1,700,000 to $2,900,000
Field hockey	15 staff	15,000	$3,000,000 to $4,000,000
Figure skating	42 staff	166,000	$7,600,000 to $35,000,00
Gymnastics	44 staff	93,000	$7,600,000 to $35,000,00
Ice hockey	40-50 staff	565,000	$7,600,000 to $35,000,00
Judo	3 staff	7,700	N/A
Karate	2 staff	12,000	N/A
Luge	21 (11 staff +10 coaches)	1,000	$1,700,000 to $2,900,000
Modern pentathlon	6 staff	1,000	N/A
Racquetball	6 staff	25,000	$1,700,000 to $2,900,000
Roller sports	7-10 staff	24,000	N/A
Rowing	12 staff	15,850	$3,000,000 to $4,000,000
Sailing	5 staff	40,000	$4,100,000 to $7,500,000
Shooting	11-16 staff	9,500	$3,000,000 to $4,000,000
Skiing	36 staff	30,000	$7,600,000 to $35,000,00
Soccer	75 staff	3,900,000	$4,100,000 to $7,500,000
Softball	15 staff	350,000	$4,100,000 to $7,500,000
Speed skating	18 staff	700	$1,700,000 to $2,900,000
Squash	1-6 staff	8,000	N/A
Swimming	50 staff	290,000	$7,600,000 to $35,000,00
Synchronized swimming	10 staff	5,500	N/A
Table tennis	5 staff	8,000	N/A

(continued)

(continued)

U.S. sport national federations	Staff size (headquarters)[1]	Membership[2]	2003 and 2004 budget[3]
Taekwondo	11 staff	30,000	$3,000,000 to $4,000,000
Team handball	3 staff	3,000	$550,000 to $1,600,000
Tennis	200-250 staff	660,000	$7,600,000 to $35,000,00
Track and field	40 staff	80,000	$7,600,000 to $35,000,00
Triathlon	15 staff	40,100	$1,700,000 to $2,900,000
Volleyball	30 staff	152,000	$4,100,000 to $7,500,000
Water polo	16 staff	35,000	N/A
Water skiing	7 staff	35,000	$1,700,000 to $2,900,000
Weightlifting	7-10 staff	3,500	$550,000 to $1,600,000
Wrestling	34 (25 staff + 9 coaches)	142,000	$4,100,000 to $7,500,000
Total		7,009,352	

[1]The staff numbers are full-time (paid) professional staff who work for the sport in administration, coaching, clerical, and so on. There are many volunteers at the regional level as well as at the local level. In most cases the regional governing bodies are not professionalized and mostly volunteer driven. The NOC (USOC) and national governing bodies (NGBs) do not receive direct U.S. governmental support. In 2001-2004 the USOC allocated $164,000,000 of high-performance funding for success at the Olympic Games. As part of the resource allocation process, each sport has to develop a High Performance Plan (HHP) with milestones and goals attached to the plan.

[2]The numbers for membership reflect actual competitors in the United States; the NGBs focus on programming, preparing athletes at all levels. The U.S. NGBs are the workhorse for the NOC; they for the most part prepare athletes for high-performance sport. For example, in the case of volleyball there are 152,000 registered players (youth, junior, and senior level). According to SGMA, the Sporting Goods Manufacturing Association, 20,286,000 of the U.S. population 6 years or older played at least once per year in 2003 (SGMA participation trends).

3Budget for NGB has been divided into five classes: $550,000 to $1,600,000; $1,700,000 to $2,900,000; $3,000,000 to $4,000,000; $4,100,000 to $7,500,000; $7,600,000 to $35,000,000.

N/A = data not available.

Source: United States Olympic Committee.

Appendix D

Olympic Sport Organisations' Performance Management Framework

OSO STRATEGIC PERFORMANCE MIX		
Governance	**Network quality**	**Economic channel**
Principles		
Decision and control processes Define strategic vision, mission, and objectives Establish evaluation and control	Capacity of the OSO's system to deliver services Capacity of the OSO's network organisations to work together	Capacity to directly or indirectly generate resources (financial, logistics...)
Tools		
Strategic planning Power distribution Evaluation system	Conventions for objectives Seal of approval Professionalization/training	Determine size of economic channel and OSO's position within it Try to position OSO in the center of its economic channel

OSO OPERATIONAL PERFORMANCE MIX Key Sucess Factors		
Professionalisation	**Organizational Culture**	**Partnerships and services**
Principles		
Capacity to realize projects and tasks defined in the strategic plan	Involment and cohesion around the OSO's strategy, work together (without conflicts)	Partnership capacity (legitimacy) and give services to stakeholders
Tools		
Level and forms of professionalization adapted to OSO's life cycle and strategic planning	Respect of history, myths, and values, Recruit "Volunteers-professionals" and "Professional-volunteers", Team building, social climate	Deliver services regarding stakeholders expectations Develop vertical, horizontal, and systemic partnerships through conventions and contracts

Key Failure Factors			
Deficient information and reporting systems	**Complexity of incentive mechanisms**	**Weak control over the actors**	**Political sclerosis**
Solutions			
Introduce strategic, managerial, and operational reporting systems Share the cost of information with stakeholders which have interest in	Global/individual Financial/non-financial (for volunteers and paid staff) linked to the strategic plan	Human resources tools: Procedures, job description, staff training, annual evaluation meeting...	Reduce gap of innovation between OSO headquarters and OSO system Avoid dysfunction in electoral system

Appendix E

Plan of the Framework for Analysing the Case Studies of the Federations (Bayle 1999)

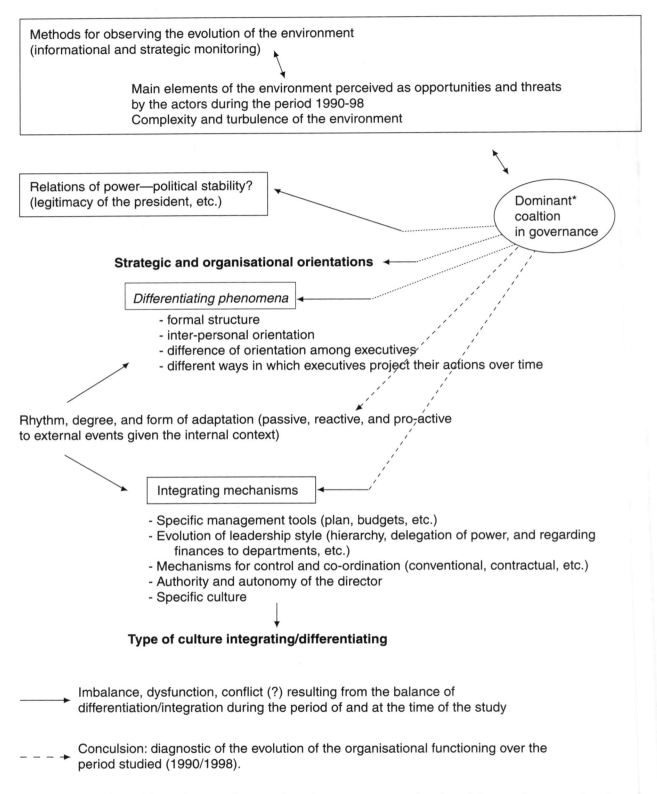

Methods for observing the evolution of the environment
(informational and strategic monitoring)

Main elements of the environment perceived as opportunities and threats
by the actors during the period 1990-98
Complexity and turbulence of the environment

Relations of power—political stability?
(legitimacy of the president, etc.)

Dominant*
coaltion
in governance

Strategic and organisational orientations

Differentiating phenomena

- formal structure
- inter-personal orientation
- difference of orientation among executives
- different ways in which executives project their actions over time

Rhythm, degree, and form of adaptation (passive, reactive, and pro-active
to external events given the internal context)

Integrating mechanisms

- Specific management tools (plan, budgets, etc.)
- Evolution of leadership style (hierarchy, delegation of power, and regarding
    finances to departments, etc.)
- Mechanisms for control and co-ordination (conventional, contractual, etc.)
- Authority and autonomy of the director
- Specific culture

Type of culture integrating/differentiating

Imbalance, dysfunction, conflict (?) resulting from the balance of
differentiation/integration during the period of and at the time of the study

Conculsion: diagnostic of the evolution of the organisational functioning over the
period studied (1990/1998).

*The leading members of the coalition can be many (president, secretary general, technical director, director, etc.) or the real authority to take decisions can be centralised and fall to a single person (i.e. the president alone in most cases with regard to statutory, legitimate authority carried out by a sole person, or the national technical director or a director general alone with regard to authority based on particularly powerful expertise and underground politics).

Bibliography

Part I References

Acosta, R.H. 2002. *Managing sport organizations.* Champaign, IL: Human Kinetics.

Ansoff, H.I. 1965. *Corporate strategy.* New York: McGraw-Hill.

Bozeman, B. 1987. *All organizations are public: bridging public and private organizational theories.* San Francisco: Jossey-Bass.

Chandler, A.D. 1962. *Strategy and structure: chapters in the history of the industrial enterprise.* Cambridge, MA: MIT Press.

Chappelet, J.L. 1991. *Le système olympique.* Grenoble: Presses universitaires.

Chappelet, J.L. 2002. L'Agence mondiale antidopage: un nouveau régulateur des relations internationales sportives. *Relations Internationales* 111: 381-401.

Chelladurai, P. 2001. *Managing organizations for sport and physical activity.* Scottsdale, AZ: Holcomb Hathaway.

CIDA. 1997. *Strategic planning: a guide for Canadian NGOs.* In collaboration with Genivar and Focus International. Published at www.focusintl.com/strategy/summary.htm.

Crozier, M. 1991. *Etat moderne, etat modeste, stratégies pour un autre changement.* Paris: Seuil.

Crozier, M., and Friedberg, E. 1977. *L'acteur et le système; les contraintes de l'action collective.* Paris: Seuil. Also trans. into English *(The actors and the system).*

Das, H. 1990. *Organization theory with Canadian application.* Toronto: Gage Educational.

Drucker, P.F. 1989, July-August. What can business learn from nonprofits. *Harvard Business Review,* pp. 88-93.

Goodstein, L., Nolan T., and Pfeiffer J. 1992. *Applied strategic planning: an introduction.* San Francisco: Jossey-Bass/Pfeiffer.

Joyce, P. 2000. *Strategy in the public sector: a guide to effective change management.* Chichester: Wiley.

Kotler, P., and Andreasen, A.R. 1991. *Strategic marketing for nonprofit organizations,* 4th ed. Englewood Cliffs, NJ: Prentice Hall.

Martinet, A.C. 1984. *Management stratégique, organisation et politique.* Paris: Ediscience International.

Mintzberg, H. 1994. *The rise and fall of strategic planning.* New York: Prentice Hall.

Mintzberg, H. 1987, July-August. Crafting Strategy. *Harvard Business Review*, pp. 66-75.

Nutt, P.C., and Backoff, R.W. 1992. *Strategic management of public and third sector organizations.* San Francisco: Jossey-Bass.

Oster, S.M. 1995. *Strategic management for nonprofit organizations: theory and cases.* New York: Oxford University Press.

Peters, T.J. 1984. Strategy follows structure: developing distinctive skills. *California Management Review* 26(3): 111-125.

Porter, M.E. 1980. *Competitive strategy: techniques for analyzing industries and competitors.* New York: Free Press.

Porter, M.E. 1995. What is strategy. *Harvard Business Review* 74(6): 61-78.

Ramanantsoa, B., and Thiery-Baslé, C. 1989. *Organisations et fédérations sportives, sociologie et management.* Paris: PUF.

Slack, T. 1997. *Understanding sport organizations.* Champaign, IL: Human Kinetics.

Thibault, L., Slack, T., and Hinings, C.R. 1993. A framework for the analysis of strategy in nonprofit sport organizations. *Journal of Sport Management* 7: 25-43.

Strategor. 1997. *Politique générale de l'entreprise.* Paris: Dunod.

Part II References

Asensi, F. 2000, April. *Rapport et propositions pour une réforme des statuts des fédérations sportives,* Sénat, Paris, www.senat.fr/rap/l00-092-331/l00-092-3317.html.

Bayle, E. 1999, November. Management et performance des organisations à but non lucratif. Le cas des fédérations sportives nationales. Thèse de doctorat de sciences de gestion, Université de Limoges.

Bayle, E. 2000, October. La mesure de la performance des organisations à but non lucratif: proposition d'une nouvelle méthode appliquée aux fédérations sportives nationales. *Revue Gestion 2000,* pp. 35-54.

Bayle, E. 2001, September. Les modalités de gouvernance des organisations à but non lucratif: une étude appliquée aux fédérations sportives nationales. *Revue des sciences de gestion,* no. 188-189 dossier ("Piloter l'entreprise"), pp. 54-69.

Bayle, E., and Camy, J. 2003. *Le dirigeant sportif fédéral aujourd'hui et demain.* Rapport pour l'Académie Olympique du CNOSF. www.cnosf.org.

Bayle, E., and Durand, C. 2000, June. Sport professionnel et représentation nationale: quel avenir? *Revue reflets and perspectives de la vie économique:* Numéro special, *Sport and mondialisation: Quel enjeu pour le XXIème siècle?* ed. J-J. Gouguet. De Boeck Université, pp. 45-59.

Brechet, J.-P. 1997. Les structures: leur importance, leur inertie, leur flexibilité. *Direction et gestion des entreprises,* no. 166, pp. 17-25.

Chappelet, J.-L. 2001. Le système olympique et les pouvoirs publics face à la corruption: partenariat ou confrontation? In *Sport et ordre public,* ed. J-C. Basson, La documentation française, pp. 215-234.

Chelladurai, P., Szyslo, M., and Haggerty, T. 1987. Systems based dimensions of effectiveness: the case of the national sport organizations. *Canadian Journal of Sport Sciences* 12: 111-119.

Chifflet, P. 1987, November 13-14. Les fédérations sportives, politiques et stratégiques. *Sciences sociales et sports: états et perspectives,* Actes des journées d'études de Strasbourg, pp. 277-287.

Desbordes, M., Ohl, F., and Tribou, G. 1999. *Marketing du sport.* Paris: Economica.

Esposito, G. Performance assessment in national sport federations: the case of the Italian track and field federation, June 2002 MEMOS, University of Lyon 1 (unpublished).

Esposito, G., and Madella, A. 2003. Quanto corre l'atletica? La valutazione della performance organizzativa della federazione italiana di atletica leggera. *Atleticastudi* no. 3-4, Management dello sport.

Fatoux, F. and Tiberghien, F. 2004, January. L'évaluation extra-financière des entreprises. *Futuribles,* no. 293, pp. 39-51.

Fitzgerald, L., Johnston, R., Brignall, S., Silvestro, R., and Voss, C. 1994. *Performance measurement in service businesses,* 3rd. ed. London: CIMA.

Frisby, W. 1986. The organizational structure and effectiveness of voluntary organizations: the case of Canadian sport governing bodies. *Journal of Park and Recreation Administration,* pp. 61-74.

Guay, D. 1997. *La culture sportive.* Paris: PUF, Pratiques corporelles.

Hall, R.H. 1980. Effectiveness theory and organizational effectiveness. *Journal of Applied Behavioral Science* 16: 536-545.

Jacquelin B. M., *Pouvoir : mythes et réalité,* Editeur Klincksieck, 1992.

Kaplan, R.S., and Norton, D.P. 1996. *Translating strategy into action: the balanced scorecard.* Boston: Harvard Business School Press. Trans. from *Le tableau de bord prospectif,* Editions d'Organisation.

Koenig, G. 1996. *Management stratégique: paradoxes, interactions et apprentissages,* coll. Connaître and pratiquer la gestion. Paris, Editions Nathan.

Koski, P. 1995. Organizational effectiveness of Finnish sports clubs. *Journal of Sport Management,* pp. 48-59.

Lawrence, P.C., and Lorsch, J. 1989. *Adapter les structures de l'entreprise; intégration ou différenciation.* Editions d'Organisation, coll. Les classiques, re-edited 1989 (1st ed. 1973, *Organization and environment,* Boston: Harvard Business School Press).

Le Duff, R., and Papillon, J.C. 1997. Gestion du non marchand. *Encyclopédie de gestion,* pp. 1605-1620.

Lorino, P. 1999, June. A la recherche de la valeur perdue: construire les processus créateurs de valeur dans le secteur public. *Revue Politiques and management public* 17(2): 21-33.

Madella, A. 1998. La performance di successo delle organizzazioni—Spunti di riflessione per gestire efficacemente le societa di atletica leggera. *Atleticastudi* 1-2-3.

Madella, A. 2001. Les paradoxes de la professionalization de la fédération italienne d'athlétisme. In *La professionalization des organisations sportives,* dir. P. Chantelat. Paris, Editions L'harmattan.

Madella, A., Carbonaro, G., Marchioni, M., and Bonagura, V. 2000. Il valore economico dell'atletica italiana. Implicazioni per la gestione dell'atletica. *Atleticastudi* 1-2, pp. 71-80.

Mahé de Boislandelle, H. 1998. Gestion des ressources humaines dans les PME. *Editions Economica,* 2nd ed., coll. Techniques de gestion.

Massiera, P. 1998. La performance sociétale: une nouvelle approche de la qualité totale? *Direction et gestion,* no. 172-173, pp. 51-58.

Mayaux, F. 1999. Typologie des conseils d'administration d'association. *Revue internationale de l'économie sociale,* no. 272, 2nd quarter, pp. 45-57.

Mintzberg, H. 1986. *Le pouvoir dans les organisations.* Paris, Editions d'organisation.

Morin, E.M., Savoie, A., and Beaudin, G. 1994. *L'efficacité de l'organisation—théories, représentations et mesures.* Montréal, Québec: Editions G. Morin.

Papadimitriou, D. 1994, September-October. How well do Greek national sport organizations do? Perceptions of organizational effectiveness based on the multiple constituency approach. *Second European Congress on Sport Management, official proceedings,* Florence, pp. 505-518.

Papadimitriou, D. 1999. Voluntary boards of directors in Greek sport governing bodies. *European Journal for Sport Management,* special issue, pp. 78-103.

Papadimitriou, D., and Taylor, P. 2000. Organizational effectiveness of Hellenic national sports organizations: a multiple constituency approach. *Sport Management Review* 3(1): 23-46.

Penrose, E. 1959. *The theory of growth of the firm.* New York: Wiley.

Pigeassou, C., and Chaze, J-P. 1999. Paradoxes and enjeux des labels dans les services sportifs: outil politique de stratégie fédérale ou vecteur dynamique de développement économique local, in actes du colloque. *Le marketing du loisir and du tourisme sportif,* dir. P. Bouchet, pp. 32-51.

Quinn R.E., and Rohrbaugh J. 1981. A competing values approach to organizational effectiveness. *Public Productivity Review* 1981, 122-140.

Quinn, R.E., and Rohrbaugh, J. 1983. A spatial model of effectiveness criteria: towards a competing values approach to organizational analysis. *Management Science* 29: 363-377.

Ramananstsoa B., and Thiery-Baslé, C. 1989. *Organisations et fédérations sportives.* Paris: PUF, Pratiques corporelles.

Romanelli, E., and Tushman, M.L. 1994. Organisational transformations as punctuated equilibrium: an empirical test. *Academy of Management Journal* 37(5): 1141-1166.

Slack, T. 1985. The bureaucratisation of a voluntary sport organization. *Review of Sociology of Sport* 20(3): 85-93. OK

Slack, T., and Thibault, L. 1988. Values and beliefs: their role in structuring of national sport organizations. *Arena Review* 12: 140-155.

Slack T., La professionnalisation des associations sportives canadiennes – Etat des recherches - in *La professionnalisation des organisations sportives* dir. P. Chantelat, Editions L'harmattan, Paris, 2001.

Spriggs, M.T. 1994. A framework for more valid measures of channel member performance. *Journal of Retailing* 70(4): 327-343.

Thibault, L., Slack, T., and Hinings, B. 1991. Professionalism, structures and systems: the impact of professional staff on voluntary organizations. *International Review for Sociology of Sport* 26(2): 83-97.

Thibault, L., Slack, T., and Hinings, B. 1994. Strategic planning for non-profit sport organizations: empirical verification of a framework. *Journal of Sport Management* 8: 218-233.

Tomé, J. Measuring the performance of swimming federations in Mediterranean countries, June 2002 MEMOS, University of Lyon 1 (unpublished).

Welch, M. 1994. The professional in a voluntary world. *Second European Congress on Sport Management,* Florence, pp. 355-367.

Part II Suggested Readings

Amis, J., and Slack, T. 1994. The pace and sequence of change in national sport organizations. *Second European Congress on Sport Management,* Florence, pp. 263-275.

Amis, J., and Slack, T. 1996. The size-structure relationship in voluntary sport organizations. *Journal of Sport Management* 10: 76-86.

Amis, J., Slack, T., and Berett, T. 1995. The structural antecedents of conflict in voluntary sport organizations. *Leisure Studies* 4: 13-26.

Atkinson, A.A., Waterhouse, J.-H., and Wells, R-B. 1997, December. Bâtir les nouveaux indicateurs de la performance globale. *L'Expansion Management Review,* pp. 78-87.

Bayle, E., and Madella, A. 2002. Development of a taxonomy of performance for national sport organizations. *European Journal of Sport Science* 2(4).

Boncler, J. 1995. Management associatif et stratégie. *Revue Internationale de l'économie sociale,* no. 255, 1st trimester, pp. 81-88.

Boulte, P. 1991. *Le diagnostic des organisations appliqué aux associations.* Paris: PUF, Le sociologue.

Bourguignon A., Peut-on définir la performance ?, *Revue française de comptabilité,* n° 269, juillet-août, 1995, pp. 61-65.

Cameron, K.S. 1984. The effectiveness of ineffectiveness, ed. B.M. Staw and L.L. Cummings, *Research in organisational behaviour* (vol. 6). Greenwich, CT: JAI Press, pp. 235-285.

Cameron, K.S., and Whetten, D.A. 1981. Perceptions of organizational effectiveness over organization life cycles. *Administrative Science Quarterly* 26: 525-544.

Chantelat, P., ed. 2001. *La professionalisation des organisations sportives.* Paris: Editions L'harmattan.

Chappelet, J-L. 2002, June. From Lake Placid to Salt Lake City: The challenging growth of the Olympic Winter Games since 1980. *European Journal of Sport Science* 2(3): 1-21.

Cruise, M.D., and Zakus, D.H. 1995. Ethical decision making in sport administration: a theoretical inquiry. *Journal of Sport Management,* pp. 36-58.

Cuskelly, G., Boag, A., and McIntyre, N. 1999. Differences in organisational commitment between paid and volunteer administrators in sport. *European Journal for Sport Management,* special issue, *Volunteers and Professionals in Sport Organisations,* pp. 39-61.

Garrabos, C., and Pigeassou, C., dir. 1997. *Management des organisations de services sportifs.* Paris: PUF.

Grayson, L.E., and Tompkins, C.J. 1984. *Management of public sector and nonprofit organizations.* Reston, VA: Reston.

Hinings, C.R., and Greenwood, R. 1988. Organizational design types, tracks, and the dynamics of strategic change. *Organization Studies* 9(3): 293-316.

Hinings, C.R., Slack, T., and Thibault, L. 1991. Professionalism, structures and systems: the impact of professional staff on voluntary sport organisations. *Review of Sociology of Sport*, pp. 33-44.

Hinings, C.R., Thibault, L., Slack, T., and Kikulis, L.M. 1996. Values and organizational structure. *Human Relations* 49(7): 885-916.

Kikulis, L. 2000. Continuity and change in decision making in national sport organizations: institutional explanations. *Journal of Sport Management* 14: 293-320.

Kikulis, L., Slack, T., and Hinings, C.R. 1992. Institutional specific design archetypes: a framework for understanding change in national sport organizations. *International Review for Sociology of Sport*, pp. 343-370.

Kikulis, L., Slack, T., and Hinings, C.R. 1995. Sector specific patterns of organizational design change. *Journal of Management Studies* 32: 67-100.

Kikulis, L., Slack, T., Hinings, C.R., and Zimmermann, A. 1989. A structural taxonomy of amateur sport organizations. *Journal of Sport Management* 3: 129-150.

Loret, A., dir. 1993. *Sport and management, de l'éthique à la pratique*. Paris: Dunod (2nd ed. 1995, Editions EPS).

Meunier, B. 1992. *Le management du non-marchand*. Paris: Editions Economica.

Mintzberg H., *Le management. Voyage au centre des organisations*, Paris, Les Editions d'Organisation, 1990.

Nizet, J. 1992. Les gestionnaires face à l'efficacité and à l'efficience. *Gestion 2000* 1, pp. 73-85.

Nizet, J., and Pichault, F. 1995. *Comprendre les organisations, Mintzberg à l'épreuve des faits*. Montréal, Québec: Editions G. Morin.

Ohana, P. 1995, December. L'art de mesurer la performance sociale. *L'expansion management review*, pp. 35-46.

Osborne, S.P. 1998. Voluntary organizations and innovation in public services. *Routledge studies in the management of voluntary and non profit organizations*. London: Routledge.

Osborne, S.P., Bovaird, A., Martin, S., and Tricker, M. 1995. Performance management and accountability in complex public programmes. *Financial Accountability Management* 11(1): 37-52.

Oster, S.M. 1995. *Strategic management for nonprofit organizations, theory and cases*. New York: Oxford University Press.

Pettigrew, A.M. 1990, August. Longtitudinal field research change: theory and practice. *Organization Science* 1(3): 267-292.

Pigeassou, C. 1993. La labellisation des activités sportives de loisirs. *Sport and management*, dir. A. Loret. Paris, Editions DUNOD, pp. 309-331.

Pujol L., *La crise des associations*, Thèse de doctorat de sciences de gestion, Université du Maine, 1995.

Pujol L., Le pouvoir au sein des associations, *Pouvoir et gestion*, 5èmes rencontres du 29 et 30 novembre 1996, *Presses de l'Université des sciences sociales de Toulouse*, 1997.

Slack, T. 1994. Theoretical diversity and the study of sport organizations. *International Review for Sociology of Sport* 29(3): 185-193.

Slack, T. 1997. *Understanding sport organizations*. Champaign, IL: Human Kinetics.

Slack, T., and Hinings, C.R. 1987. Dynamics of quadriennal plan implementation in national sport organizations. *The organization and administration of sport*, ed. T. Slack and C.R. Hinings. London, Ontario: Sports Dynamics, pp. 42-63.

Slack, T., and Hinings, C.R. 1987. Planning and organizational change: a conceptual framework for the analysis of amateur sport organizations. *Canadian Journal of Applied Sciences* 12: 185-193.

Slack, T., and Hinings, B. 1992. Understanding change in national sport organizations: an integration of theoretical perspectives. *Journal of Sport Management* 6: 114-132.

Theodoraki, E.I., and Henry, I.P. 1994. Organisational structures and contexts, British national governing bodies of sport. *International Review for Sociology of Sport* 29(3).

Thery, H. 1987. L'association est-elle une entreprise comme les autres? *Associations and activités économiques*. Paris: approche juridique, uniops, pp. 50-71.

Thibault, L., Slack, T., and Hinings, B. 1993. A framework for the analysis of strategy in non-profit sport organizations. *Journal of Sport Management* 7: 25-43.

Tribou, G., and Auge, B. 2003. Management du sport. *Marketing et gestion des clubs sportifs*. Paris: Dunod.

Vail S.E., *Organizational effectiveness and national sport governing bodies : a constituency approach*, Université d'Ottawa, PHD Thesis (unpublished), 1986.

Van hoecke, J., and de Knop, P. 1998. IKGym: a model for evaluating Flemish gymnastics clubs. *European Journal for Sport Management*, special issue, *Service Quality*, pp. 23-39.

Wilson, D.C., and Butler R.J. 1990. *Managing the nonprofit organization*. London: Butterworth, Heinemann.

Wittock, H., Laporte, W., and Meerbeek, R.V. 1996. The development of an instrument with which sports federations can evaluate and optimize their management. *European Journal for Sport Management*, no. 1, pp. 90-101.